MW00799506

Principles of Biblical Interpretation in the Lutheran Confessions

Revised Edition

Principles of Biblical Interpretation in the Lutheran Confessions

Revised Edition

RALPH A. BOHLMANN

Publishing House
St. Louis

Copyright © 1968, 1983 Concordia Publishing House
3558 S. Jefferson Avenue, St. Louis, MO 63118
Manufactured in the United States of America

All rights reserved. No part of this publication may be reproduced, stored in a retrieval system, or transmitted, in any form or by any means, electronic, mechanical, photocopying, recording, or otherwise, without the prior written permission of Concordia Publishing House.

Library of Congress Cataloging in Publication Data

Bohlmann, Ralph A.
    Principles of biblical interpretation in the Lutheran confessions.

    Bibliography: p.
    Includes index.
    1. Bible—Criticism, interpretation, etc.—History.
2. Lutheran Church—Catechisms and creeds—History and criticism. I. Title.
BS500.B6 1983   220.6   83-7830
ISBN 0-570-03910-X

2 3 4 5 6 7 8 9 10   CB   91 90 89 88 87 86 85 84 83

Contents

List of Abbreviations

AC—Augsburg Confession
Ap—Apology of the Augsburg Confession
Ep—Epitome of the Formula of Concord
FC—Formula of Concord
LC—Large Catechism
SA—Smalcald Articles
SC—Small Catechism
SD—Solid Declaration of the Formula of Concord
Tr—Treatise on the Power and Primacy of the Pope

Uppercase Roman numerals following the above abbreviations denote article numbers, except in the Smalcald Articles, where they refer to parts. In the Smalcald Articles, article numbers are indicated by lowercase Roman numerals. Arabic numerals following Roman numerals identify the paragraph or paragraphs from which the citation is taken.

Preface to the Revised Edition

The subject matter of this volume was initially treated in a modest essay delivered to a meeting of seminary faculties and District presidents of The Lutheran Church—Missouri Synod in November 1965. That meeting, like several gatherings of those churchmen in the early '60s, was concerned with the increasing indications that some synodical theologians were employing the historical-critical method of Biblical interpretation, and, predictably, reaching and teaching conclusions at variance with synodical positions.

In that context, a major impetus for dealing with the issue was to refute the often-advanced claim that the Lutheran Confessions, because they have no specific article on the nature and authority of Holy Scripture, therefore have no doctrine of Scripture. The implication of that faulty claim, then and now, is that Lutheran subscription to the historic confessions does not bind its churches or theologians to any particular understanding of the nature, authority, and interpretation of Scripture. In that view, Lutheran theologians are supposedly free to discard traditional attitudes toward the Scriptures in favor of a more contemporary historical-critical approach. But the raw data of the confessions, carefully and honestly observed, make it abundantly clear that the confessions do in fact set forth and employ a consistent understanding of the nature, authority, and interpretation of Holy Scripture, and that they do so for theological reasons. To subscribe to the Lutheran Confessions in any strong and meaningful way is also to subscribe to their view of Holy Scripture and its proper interpretation.

No one needs to understand that better than the pastors of the Lutheran Church, and the sooner in their seminary education the better! This volume was prepared primarily to assist seminary students to that end. For that reason, its format consists essen-

11

tially in the clustering of citations from the confessional writings on various aspects of Biblical authority and interpretation. It does not often present the historical context of those citations, analyze them, or apply them to ancient or contemporary problems. It is a handbook for students, and it deals with basics; it is not primarily a reference work for professors! But it is precisely in such basics that commitment is most critically needed today! For that reason, pastors and professors, no less than students and interested laymen, may also find these pages to be an informative and useful compendium of basic Lutheran affirmations about the Word of God. Perhaps others will build upon these basic emphases by undertaking more analytical and comprehensive studies of the principles and practice of confessional Biblical interpretation.

The author expresses his deep appreciation to the editorial staff of Concordia Publishing House and especially to Ruth Ann Johnson and David Lumpp for their considerable assistance in preparing this revised edition. It has eliminated or translated most of the Latin and German references of the first edition and updated several of the references. Its primary difference from the first edition is the addition of a new concluding chapter that applies the principles of confessional Biblical interpretation to the contemporary problem of historical-critical interpretation. Like the earlier chapters, it is designed to help students of the Word understand and appreciate the close connection between Holy Scripture as the Word of God and the primary mission of the church to confess and proclaim the Gospel of Jesus Christ.

The German poet Goethe reminded us that what we have inherited from our fathers must be acquired before it can be possessed. Sad to say, contemporary Lutheran attitudes toward Holy Scripture and its interpretation too often reveal an astonishing neglect, confusion, or even denial of the confessional approach to Holy Scripture. For our sake and that of the church, may God help us to acquire and possess what our fathers in the faith have bequeathed to us in the Lutheran Confessions concerning the Word of God and its interpretation.

Ralph A. Bohlmann
Eastertide 1983

The Lutheran Confessions As Biblical Expositions

Subscription to the 16th-century Lutheran Confessions is a common characteristic of all major bodies in world Lutheranism today. To be sure, there is something less than full agreement among Lutherans as to both the quantitative and qualitative significance of this subscription. Some Lutherans, like those of The Lutheran Church—Missouri Synod, subscribe to all the confessions contained in the *Book of Concord* of 1580.[1] Other Lutherans limit their subscription to some of the earlier 16th-century confessions.[2] Likewise, there have been differences of opinion on the binding nature of confessional subscription for the contemporary church. Some Lutherans understand their subscription to bind them to the doctrinal content of the confessions *because* this content is drawn from Holy Scripture, but others have subscribed to the confessions only *insofar as* they conform to Holy Scripture. Still others have accepted the confessions as having only historical validity; that is, they accept the confessions as valid answers to problems faced when they were written but suggest that the church of today may well have to give different answers to contemporary problems. Important and crucial though these different understandings of confessional subscription are, they do not obscure the fact that for world Lutheranism today the Lutheran Confessions continue to provide the definitive doctrinal answer to the question: What is Lutheran?

With their subscription to the Lutheran Confessions, Lutherans have not, however, established an independent doctrinal standard with a function similar to that of tradition in Tridentine

Roman Catholicism. Although the word "and" in the frequently employed formulation "Scripture and the Confessions" may give the erroneous impression that Lutherans have two doctrinal standards, the official statements of Lutheran bodies make it quite clear that the confessions are accepted and have authority only because they are expositions and summaries of Holy Scripture, which remains the only source and norm for faith and life. Thus the constitution of The Lutheran Church—Missouri Synod states that this body accepts "all the Symbolical Books of the Evangelical Lutheran Church as a true and unadulterated statement and exposition of the Word of God."[3] At their ordination, pastors of this denomination accept the three ecumenical creeds "as faithful testimonies to the truth of the Holy Scriptures"; they state their belief that the Unaltered Augsburg Confession is "a true exposition of the Word of God" and that the remaining confessions in the *Book of Concord* "are also in agreement with this one Scriptural faith."[4]

Similarly, other branches of Lutheranism accept the confessions as expositions of Holy Scripture. The American Lutheran Church, which began its organizational existence January 1, 1961, as a result of the merger of the American Lutheran Church, the Evangelical Lutheran Church, and the United Evangelical Lutheran Church, accepts and confesses the ancient ecumenical creeds, the Unaltered Augsburg Confession, and Luther's Small Catechism "as brief and true statements of the doctrines of the Word of God" and recognizes the later Lutheran Confessions "as normative for its theology." It "accepts without reservation" the Lutheran symbolical books "not insofar as but because they are the presentation and explanation of the pure doctrine of the Word of God and a summary of the faith of the evangelical Lutheran Church."[5]

The Lutheran Church in America, formed in 1962 by the union of the United Lutheran Church in America, the American Evangelical Lutheran Church, the Finnish Evangelical Lutheran Church (Suomi Synod), and the Augustana Lutheran Church, sees the Lutheran Confessions not as norms independent of Holy Scripture, but as witnesses to the Gospel transmitted by the Scriptures. This Lutheran body accepts the three ecumenical

14

creeds "as true declarations of the faith of the Church," the Unaltered Augsburg Confession and Luther's Small Catechism "as true witnesses to the Gospel," and the other Lutheran Confessions in the *Book of Concord* "as further valid interpretations of the confession of the Church." In a summary statement, the Lutheran Church in America affirms "that the Gospel transmitted by the Holy Scriptures, to which the creeds and confessions bear witness, is the true treasure of the Church, the substance of its proclamation, and the basis of its unity and continuity."[6]

The role of the Lutheran Confessions as expositions of Holy Scripture is clearly stated in the constitution of the Lutheran World Federation as well:

> The Lutheran World Federation acknowledges the Holy Scriptures of the Old and New Testaments as the only source and the infallible norm of all church doctrine and practice, and sees in the three Ecumenical Creeds and in the Confessions of the Lutheran Church, especially in the Unaltered Augsburg Confession and Luther's Small Catechism, a pure exposition of the Word of God.[7]

Following the above citation nearly verbatim, the constitution of the Lutheran Council in the United States of America notes that the participating Lutheran church bodies "see in" the Lutheran Confessions "a pure exposition of the Word of God."[8]

Still other illustrations from the world of Lutheranism could be cited to show that Lutheran churches today accept their historic confessions as expositions of Holy Scripture. In this understanding of the expository function of the confessions with reference to Holy Scripture, contemporary Lutherans are continuing to reflect the confessions' own self-understanding. The classical confessional statement on this self-understanding is the following:

> Other symbols and other writings are not judges like Holy Scripture, but merely witnesses and expositions of the faith, setting forth how at various times the Holy Scriptures were understood in the church of God by contemporaries with reference to controverted articles, and how contrary teachings were rejected and condemned (FC Ep Rule and Norm, 8).[9]

15

Earlier it is stated that such writings "should be received in no other way and no further than as witnesses to the fashion in which the doctrine of the prophets and apostles was preserved in post-apostolic times" (FC Ep Rule and Norm, 2). The confessions are "a summary formula and pattern, unanimously approved, in which the summarized doctrine commonly confessed by the churches of the pure Christian religion is drawn together out of the Word of God" (FC SD Rule and Norm, 1).

The dependence of individual confessional documents on Holy Scripture is also clearly stated. The ancient creeds are understood to be the true Christian doctrine as it was correctly and soundly understood in ancient times and "drawn together out of God's Word in brief articles or chapters against the aberrations of heretics" (FC SD Rule and Norm, 4). Luther calls the Catechism "a brief compend and summary of all the Holy Scriptures" (LC Longer Preface, 18) and even maintains that in the first three chief parts of the Catechism "everything contained in Scripture is comprehended in short, plain, and simple terms" (LC Shorter Preface, 18). Similarly the Formula of Concord says of Luther's catechisms: "They are 'the layman's Bible' and contain everything which Holy Scripture discusses at greater length and which a Christian must know for his salvation" (FC Ep Rule and Norm, 5). Like the other confessions, the catechisms "formulate Christian doctrine on the basis of God's Word" (FC SD Rule and Norm, 8).

The preface to the Augsburg Confession claims that this confession is taught "on the basis of divine and holy Scripture" (AC Preface, 8), and the conclusion to the first part maintains that the preceding articles agree with "the pure Word of God and Christian truth" and that they are "grounded clearly on the Holy Scriptures." The later authors of the Formula of Concord therefore maintained that the truth of God's Word, brought to light through the ministry of Martin Luther and "drawn from and conformed to the Word of God, is summarized in the articles and chapters of the Augsburg Confession against the aberrations of the papacy and of other sects." They declared their adherence to the Augsburg Confession "as our symbol in this epoch, not because this confession was prepared by our theologians but

16

because it is taken from the Word of God and solidly and well grounded therein" (FC SD Rule and Norm, 5).

The Biblical expository nature of the confessions is nowhere in greater evidence than in Melanchthon's Apology of the Augsburg Confession, where copious citations and explanations of Biblical texts are found in nearly every article. Melanchthon begins the Apology with the claim that this document will demonstrate to the reader that "far from having disproved our contentions from the Scriptures, they [the Roman Catholic opponents] have condemned several articles in opposition to the clear Scripture of the Holy Spirit" (Ap Preface, 9), and he concludes on the same note (Ap XXVIII, 27). The writers of the Formula of Concord therefore unanimously pledged their adherence to the Apology not only because it clearly expounded and defended the Augsburg Confession, but also "because it is supported with clear and irrefutable testimonies from the Holy Scriptures" (FC SD Rule and Norm, 6).

In the Smalcald Articles Luther constantly appeals to the Bible over against all other authorities such as popes and church fathers. St. Augustine does not write that there is a purgatory "nor does he cite any passages of the Scriptures that would constrain him to adopt such an opinion." No, "it will not do to make articles of faith out of the holy Fathers' words or works. . . . This means that the Word of God shall establish articles of faith and no one else, not even an angel" (SA II, ii, 15). Thus the Formula of Concord can assert not only that the doctrine of the Augsburg Confession is repeated in the Smalcald Articles, but also that "several articles are further explained on the basis of God's Word" (FC SD Rule and Norm, 7).

The authors of the Formula of Concord basically did not regard their task as the writing of "a different or a new confession of our faith" but as pledging themselves again "to those public and well-known symbols or common confessions which have at all times and in all places been accepted in all the churches of the Augsburg Confession before the outbreak of the several controversies" (FC SD Rule and Norm, 2). They are convinced that

the Christian reader who really delights in the truth of God's

Word will find in the previously mentioned writings what he should accept as correct and true in each of the controverted articles of our Christian faith, according to the prophetic and apostolic writings of God's Word, and what he should reject, flee, and avoid as false and wrong (FC SD Rule and Norm, 16).

The purpose of the Formula of Concord is, on the basis of Holy Scripture and the earlier confessions,

to set forth and explain our faith and confession unequivocally, clearly, and distinctly in theses and antitheses, opposing the true doctrine to the false doctrine, so that the foundation of divine truth might be made apparent in every article and that every incorrect, dubious, suspicious, and condemned doctrine might be exposed, no matter where or in what books it might be found or who may have said it or supported it (FC SD Rule and Norm, 19).

Thus the Formula of Concord sees itself not only as Biblical exposition but also as an exposition of the earlier Biblically based confessions, especially the Augsburg Confession. Thus the Preface to the *Book of Concord* states that the Formula of Concord was subscribed to because it "was agreeable and conformable first of all to the Word of God and then to the Augsburg Confession as well." The Formula was prepared "on the basis of God's Word"; its tenets were discussed "in extensive writings based on God's Word"; earlier drafts were "fortified with the Word of God against all sorts of perilous misunderstanding." The authors of the Formula are certain of their Christian confession and faith "on the basis of the divine, prophetic and apostolic Scriptures"; their explanation is "thoroughly grounded in God's Word," and their agreement is "based on the prophetic and apostolic Scriptures." [10]

Because the confessions see themselves as well as the three ecumenical creeds as expositions of the Holy Scriptures, they do not regard themselves as a second norm standing alongside of Scripture. They are rather explanations, summaries, and restatements of the truths of Scripture, which remains the sole doctrinal standard. Helmut Echternach expresses this relationship very well:

18

What is confession? Confession stands over against Scripture as the answer of the church to the speaking of God. In confession the church repeats to her Lord in worship and praise what He first said in the Bible. It is thus dialog and liturgy.[11]

Yet it is precisely this relationship to the Scriptures that gives the confessions themselves a normative role in the life of the church. The Formula states:

Our intention was only to have a single, universally accepted, certain, and common form of doctrine which all our Evangelical churches subscribe and from which and according to which, because it is drawn from the Word of God, all other writings are to be approved and accepted, judged and regulated (FC SD Rule and Norm, 10).[12]

It is to be noted that the verbs in the closing words of the citation assign the same functions to the confessions that earlier had been given to the Scriptures.[13] How can a confession judge and regulate other writings when these functions belong to the Scriptures as the *only* true norm" (FC SD Rule and Norm, 3; italics added)? The answer lies in the statement quoted above, "because it is drawn from the Word of God." The confessions, as expositions, restatements, or summaries of Holy Scripture, have a normative function only because of this relationship. The confessions are not an independent norm; they rather share in the normative function of Scripture. The Formula explains:

No one can blame us if we derive our expositions and decisions in the controverted articles from these writings, for just as we base our position on the Word of God as the eternal truth, so we introduce and cite these writings as a witness to the truth (FC SD Rule and Norm, 13).

The understanding of the confessions as Biblical exposition is of great importance to a confessional and confessing church. Edmund Schlink has stated this very well:

Confessions in their proper sense will never be taken seriously until they are taken seriously as exposition of the Scriptures, to be specific, as the church's exposition of the Scriptures. Confessions are not free-lancing theological opinions; they are

19

statements of doctrine that must be understood even to their last detail in terms of that exposition of Scripture which is the church's responsibility entrusted to it in and with the responsibility of proclamation.[14]

As Schlink points out, "Every structural analysis of the Confessions must start with their constantly emphasized expository dependence on Holy Writ."[15] Thus a legitimate stand over against the Lutheran Confessions is possible only by retracing their exegesis of Scripture, not only of the passages of Scripture cited in the confessions but of all relevant statements of Holy Scripture. Only on the basis of such an exegetical investigation and the subsequent comparison of its results with the confessions can the confessions be honestly accepted or rejected, as Schlink states: "Since the Confessions insist on being recognized as exposition of Scripture, only that response takes them seriously which affirms or rejects them on the basis of Scripture."[16]

The aforementioned exegetical-confessional investigation is not the purpose of this book. Some preliminary studies of this kind are already in existence, although the need for a broad comprehensive study of this nature remains.[17] Moreover, it is assumed that those who subscribe to the Lutheran Confessions at their ordination and installation have already made such an investigation and will continue to study the Biblical adequacy of the confessions throughout their ministry.

Basic and preliminary to the above investigation, however, is an understanding of the principles of Biblical interpretation employed in the Lutheran Confessions. The setting forth of these principles and the presuppositions on which they rest is the primary purpose of this book. In our investigation we shall give primary attention to confessional statements referring explicitly to Biblical interpretation and to examples of Biblical interpretation within the confessions that illustrate hermeneutical principles.[18]

The principles for interpreting any piece of literature are to a large extent determined by the nature, content, and purpose of that literature. This maxim is especially true for the principles of

Biblical interpretation employed in the Lutheran Confessions. Accordingly, in our first part we shall set forth the confessional view of the form, functions, fundamental clarity, and central content of Holy Scripture. In a sense, these topics indicate the presuppositions of Biblical interpretation for the Lutheran Confessions.

In our second part we shall set forth various principles of historical-grammatical exegesis employed in the confessions, and investigate the role played by the Law-Gospel distinction, the doctrine of justification by grace, and ecclesiastical tradition in the confessional interpretation of Holy Scripture. Our conclusion will summarize the major results of our investigation and suggest implications for the task of Biblical interpretation in the confessing church of today.

Certain limitations on the scope of our research have been necessary. We are not investigating in detail pre-Reformation hermeneutical principles, something that would be most helpful in understanding the continuity or discontinuity of the methodology of ecclesiastical Biblical interpretation in the Reformation era. Our investigation of the nonconfessional writings of the authors of the Lutheran Confessions has also been limited to a few representative books and statements. The author recognizes a need for a comprehensive investigation in this area, although caution must also be used in drawing conclusions from private writings with reference to confessional positions, "since authors of public documents of the church may have been restrained from expressing in such documents opinions which they felt at complete liberty to voice in their private writings."[19]

Our research in the confessions is based on the original languages of these documents. Our citations of the confessions in this paper are limited, however, to the official texts of each document. In the interest of greater readability, we are quoting the confessions from the English translations contained in the *Book of Concord,* unless otherwise noted.[20] Because of their number, the references for the confessional citations in this book will normally be indicated in parentheses following the citation. These references employ the abbreviations identified on page 9.

Finally, it should be noted that we have made little attempt to incorporate quotations from many secondary sources on the Lutheran Confessions. The secondary sources cited are quoted either because of their valuable insights or their current popularity. This restraint in the use of secondary sources stems from the author's conviction that the Lutheran Confessions speak more eloquently and clearly when they speak for themselves.

PART I

The Confessional View of Holy Scripture

CHAPTER 1

The Form
of Holy Scripture

Preliminary Considerations

The attitude of an interpreter toward the nature of Holy Scripture will materially influence his principles of Biblical interpretation. If the Scriptures are regarded as some sort of esoteric language, the interpreter is likely to follow some rather bizarre interprtative techniques. If he sees the Scriptures merely as the word of men written at different times and in different languages, he will adopt only such interpretative techniques as are common to the exposition of any piece of literature. If, on the other hand, he sees the Scriptures as God's own Word, his interpretative technique will reflect this unique factor. It is important, therefore, that we endeavor to understand the confessional view of the form of Holy Scripture.

A student of the confessions is struck by the absence of an article on this subject in the *Book of Concord,* particularly when he realizes that there were precedents for the inclusion of such an article. *The Ansbach Evangelical Counsel* of Sept. 30, 1524, not only contains statements about the proper interpretation of Holy Scripture, but begins with a short treatment of the divine authority of Holy Scripture. These Lutheran confessors state that they intend to base all articles in their confession

> on the clear, bright, and pure Word of God ... and to let nothing
> guide or direct us, through human precepts or opinion, from the
> same eternal Word of God which alone saves and, as Christ
> witnesses, abides forever, with no letter or tittle to fall from it.[1]

The basis of Biblical authority is stated a few paragraphs later, namely, that "the apostles and evangelists spoke and wrote not on their own but by the Holy Spirit."[2] This statement is supported by the citation of Matt. 10:20; Mark 13:11; Acts 1:8; 2:4; 1 Peter 1:12; and 2 Peter 1:20. The article continues:

> Inasmuch as all holy apostles spoke and wrote, as was mentioned, by the Holy Spirit alone and became Christ's witnesses to the end of the earth, so their writings cannot be human fabrication, lost or perverted, but of necessity they most certainly must remain without doubt.[3]

While the exact author or authors of this statement remain unknown, Schmidt makes the judgment that "The Ansbach theology is also substantively a segment of the thought world of Luther."[4]

Later in 1524 *The First Nuernberg Evangelical Counsel* included a lengthy article near the beginning that bore the title "What God's Word Is as to Its Right, Ground, and Origin".[5] In 1528 *"The Twenty-three Nuernberg Articles of Inquiry,"* intended primarily for use in church visitations, had as their first article a treatment entitled "On Doctrine and Holy Scripture".[6] Likewise, the *Copenhagen Articles* of 1530 begin with the statement that canonical Scripture is the sole rule and law according to which all those who want to receive grace and salvation from God must live and be governed.[7]

The absence of a special confessional article on Holy Scripture becomes still more striking when one recalls not only the many interpretations of Scripture prevalent in Luther's day and before, but also the importance that the article on Holy Scripture has for all other articles of the Christian faith. Some writers have attempted to explain this absence. Schlink, for example, states:

> One might think that this silence of the Confessions could be explained by the fact that the doctrine of inspiration was at that time the common theological heritage of the Reformers and of Roman and other opponents, even of Sebastian Franck, for example. When one considers, however, what manifold possibilities in terms of doctrines of inspiration were already present at the time of the Reformation, having been prepared by the Middle Ages, and what far-reaching consequences the decisions in the doctrine of inspiration have for other articles of

dogmatics, then this reticence cannot be accidental, but must be taken seriously as a theological decision. At any rate, the normative position of Scripture is not deduced from doctrinal statements about the divine inspiration of Scripture.[8]

What "theological decision" does Schlink have in mind? Earlier he explains:

> The absence of such an article in the Augsburg Confession is not to be construed as an evasion of the controversial problem of the relationship between Scripture and tradition. Rather, it reflects the genuinely Lutheran urgency of coming to grips at once with the *viva vox evangelii,* an approach that goes beyond the Ansbach biblicism.[9]

Schlink concludes that for the confessions "the Gospel is the norm in Scripture and Scripture is the norm for the sake of the Gospel."[10] For Schlink, the "theological decision" of the confessions on this matter is that the authority of Scripture is grounded on the Gospel, not on a doctrine of inspiration; to have emphasized the latter may have obscured the former.

Werner Elert's explanation deserves careful consideration. After explaining how the doctrine of justification is the key to Luther's Scripture principle, Elert continues:

> This explains early Lutheranism's initial stand with regard to the Scriptural principle. The fact that the Augsburg Confession says nothing about this principle shows that it recognizes Luther's position with respect to Scripture. Had it begun with special statements about Scripture—say, that Scripture is God's Word, that it is inspired, that it is necessary for the knowledge of God and salvation—this would have been wasted effort over against the Roman opposition. Rome did not question any of these statements. The declaration "Nothing but Christ should be preached" was what gave the Scriptural principle as defined by Lutheranism its truly reformational character. On the other hand, it was not possible to formulate this as if it were in opposition to the conception of Scripture as this conception, expressed in the aforementioned statements, was the common property of medieval theology. Objectively speaking, it was not in opposition. Nor were the writers of the confessions convinced that it was. Consequently, it was neces-

sary to presuppose the traditional Scriptural principle as a self-evident, common basis and, by means of a Christological treatment in all details, to establish what was specifically reformational. This was done in the whole soteriological position of the Augsburg Confession, in the Apology, and, in addition, in Luther's Smalcald Articles.[11]

In short, Elert, like Schlink, emphasizes the soteriological character of the confessional doctrine of Scripture. He emphasizes more clearly than Schlink, however, that belief in the divine authorship of Scripture was common to Lutherans and Roman Catholics alike.

F. E. Mayer enumerates three reasons for the absence of a specific article in the Lutheran Confessions dealing with Holy Scripture. First, he points out,

> The Medieval Western Church had never questioned the divine inspiration and authority of the canonical writings of the Old and the New Testament. In their conflict with Rome the Lutherans could take for granted that they and their opponents accepted the Bible as God's Word.[12]

Second, Mayer points to the fact that symbolics "deals with actual life situations and makes no attempt to present the Christian faith in every point nor in a systematic and comprehensive manner."[13] Third, Mayer contends,

> The Lutheran Confessions have no specific article on the divine character of Scripture, because their interest was centered so prominently on a Christocentric approach to Scripture. They have no interest in an atomistic, prooftext, concordance approach to Scripture.... Without the knowledge of the Gospel the Bible remains a meaningless and useless book .... The Lutheran Confessions take for granted that a Christian accepts the Scriptures as God's Word, both as God speaking in this Word here and now and as God's Word spoken in times past through the holy writers.[14]

In other words, Mayer, like Elert and Schlink, emphasizes the Christological approach to Scripture in the confessions, although he also maintains that the belief in the divine inspiration of Holy Scripture is a factor in the confessional doctrine of Scripture.

That the confessions approach Scripture Christologically can hardly be denied, as we shall demonstrate in Chapter 5. But that this Christological emphasis explains the absence of a doctrinal article on Scripture may be questioned. There is simply no evidence in the confessions or elsewhere to support the idea that the omission of an article or articles on Holy Scripture in favor of a Christological approach to Scripture was a conscious "theological decision," as Schlink maintains and Elert and Mayer imply. We do know, however, that belief in the divine inspiration, infallibility, and authority of Holy Scripture was common property of Roman Catholic, Lutheran, Reformed, and other parties involved in the controversies dealt with in the Lutheran Confessions. Since church confessions normally deal primarily with controverted articles, there was no pressing need for an article on Holy Scripture. Arthur Carl Piepkorn states simply:

> If there was one point of universal agreement among all of these [Calvin, Tridentine decrees, pre-Reformation Scholasticism] aside from the nude assertions of the Ecumenical Creeds, it was the authority, the inspiration, and the inerrancy of the Sacred Scriptures. It is not surprising, therefore, that we do not have an explicit article on the Sacred Scriptures in the Lutheran Symbols.[15]

Similarly, Holsten Fagerberg states, "When the Confessions were written, the authority of the Bible was not a problem; its authority was recognized on both sides of the confessional line of demarcation."[16]

That all parties to the 16th-century controversies dealt with in the Lutheran Confessions acknowledged the divine authority of Holy Scripture rests on another commonly held doctrinal position: that the primary author of Holy Scripture is God Himself. Divine authorship and divine authority were inseparable concepts for the Lutheran confessors. One who would understand their attitude on this point must be familiar enough with their nonconfessional writings to realize this basic position. Our investigation is confined primarily to the statements of the confessions themselves, but studies by others have emphasized that the Lutheran confessors grounded the divine authority of Holy Scripture in its divine authorship. One respected investigation of Luther's attitude toward Scripture, for example, concludes with these words:

> And, indeed, as long as the divine authority of the Bible is maintained, and as long as it is conceded that it is the product of a unique cooperation of the Holy Spirit and the human writers and, therefore, as a whole and in all its details the Word of God without contradiction and error, so long the question after the mode of inspiration is of an entirely secondary nature, and so long one is in harmony with the best Lutheran theologians from Luther up to the year 1570.[17]

Before we analyze the confessional statements of the form of Holy Scripture, however, we should briefly examine another preliminary question: the extent of the Biblical canon for the Lutheran Confessions. One might expect to find a treatment of this question in the confessions for a number of reasons. For one thing, it is well known that Luther had expressed doubts regarding the canonicity of several Biblical books. In 1522, for example, he did not regard the books of Hebrews, James, Jude, and Revelation as canonical. Earlier he had regarded the Old Testament apocryphal writings as canonical.[18] One might well have expected confessional clarification on the canonical status of these books. Moreover, other denominational confessions of the 16th century, like the *Canons and Decrees of the Council of Trent* and some Reformed confessions, expressed themselves on this question.[19] Contrary to such expectations, however, one does not find an answer to this question in the Lutheran Confessions.

The confessions do not work with the concept of canonicity, nor do they describe the Scriptures as "canonical." Instead, designations such as "the prophetic and apostolic writings of the Old and New Testaments" (FC Ep Rule and Norm, 1) or the "Holy Scriptures of God" (FC SD V, 3) are employed. As Schlink correctly states, "A criticism of the canon of Scripture or even an intracanonical criticism in the light of the Gospel, though not expressly excluded, is nowhere undertaken."[20]

An attempt to determine which books are canonical by an examination of their use in the confessions is likewise inconclusive. On the one hand, one notes that the confessions do not quote or cite Joshua, Judges, Ruth, 2 Kings, Ezra, Nehemiah, Esther, Song of Solomon, Lamentations, Joel, Amos, Obadiah, Micah, Nahum, Zephaniah, Haggai, 3 John, or Jude.[21] But they *do* cite or allude to passages from books about which Luther had expressed some misgivings: James is employed 15 times, Hebrews 37 times, and Revelation 8 times.[22] Most strikingly, the confessions refer to two of the Old Testament apocryphal writings without questioning their canonicity. These references occur in Melanchthon's Apology. His references to Tobit 4:5, 11, and 19 are in answer to an interpretation given these passages by the Roman Catholic *Confutation* (Ap IV, 277—279). That he does not discuss the canonicity of Tobit is no doubt caused by his desire to remain with the main issue he is treating: the doctrine of justification by grace. Melanchthon's reference to 2 Maccabees 15:14 is casual: "Nevertheless, there is no passage in Scripture about the dead praying, except for the dream recorded in the Second Book of the Maccabees"(Ap XXI, 9). Again, Melanchthon does not include the question of canonicity in his argumentation.

One cannot argue for the definitive extent of the canon on the basis of the Lutheran Confessions, therefore. The chief reason for the absence of statements on this issue lies in the nature of the documents in the *Book of Concord* and in their intended purposes. The earlier Lutheran Confessions were primarily intended to clarify the Lutheran doctrine of justification on the basis of Scripture, or in the case of the catechisms, to discuss briefly the chief points of Christian doctrine. That the Formula of Concord, written after the Council of Trent, does not contain a list of canonical books is not surprising when one remembers its primary concern to settle intra-Lutheran difficulties, of which the extent of the Biblical canon was not one. The absence of a canonical list does indicate, however, that for the Lutheran Confessions this was not held to be a theological problem of the first magnitude, there being general consensus as to which books should be included among the prophetic and apostolic Scriptures of the Old and New Testaments.

Holy Scripture as the Written Word of God

Although there is no specific article on the nature of Holy Scripture in the Lutheran Confessions, there are numerous statements and concepts that indicate clearly that the confessors regard the Scriptures as the inspired Word of God. We shall first analyze various statements of the confessions, then the concepts "Word of God," "command of God," and "divine law." Finally, we shall comment on the "humanity" of Holy Scripture as evidenced in the Lutheran Confessions.

Of primary importance for the confessional, yes, catholic, view of Holy Scripture is the statement of the Nicene Creed: "And in the Holy Spirit . . . who spoke by the prophets."[23] Remembering that the Lutheran Confessions accept the three ecumenical creeds as possessing the highest authority,"[24] this statement is especially significant. The phrase, which is a part of the Third Article associated with the Nicene Creed from the time of the Council of Constantinople, A.D. 381, is found in other early literature and creeds, for example, the ancient creed of Jerusalem.[25] Kelly remarks that these words had a long history in creeds and went back to the primitive kerygma of Christendom."[26] The phrase expresses in language similar to 2 Peter 1:21 the Scriptural teaching on the inspiration of "holy men of God." It expresses both the divine and the human authorship of the Scriptures. Thus the Lutheran Confessions take their stand with the ancient and modern church that confesses this catholic understanding of Biblical authorship.

The divine nature of Holy Scripture is evident in a number of places in the *Book of Concord* as well. We note, first of all, how this is expressed by the frequent use of adjectives or phrases modifying "Scriptures." The Preface of the Augsburg Confession states that the Augustana sets forth what the Lutherans were preaching and teaching "on the basis of the Holy Scriptures";[27] the Conclusion similarly ends with the offer to provide further information "on the basis of the divine Holy Scripture." A reader of the Preface to the *Book of Concord* is struck by the frequency with which the word "divine" is used to modify either "Scriptures" or "Word,"[28] and how often the contents of the confessions drawn from Scripture are characterized as "divine truth."[29] The Bible is called "the Holy Scripture of God (FC SD V, 3). Melanchthon's descriptive reference to the Scriptures in the Preface of the Apology is still more precise in referring Biblical authorship to the Holy Spirit. He there maintains that his Roman Catholic opponents have "condemned several articles in opposition to the clear Scripture of the Holy Spirit" (Ap Preface, 9).

Granted that references to the Scriptures as "divine" or "of the Holy Spirit" *may* not be explicitly stating divine *authorship,* there are confessional statements that do. In the Apology, amazed that his opponents "are unmoved by the many passages in the Scriptures that clearly attribute justification to faith and specifically deny it to works," Melanchthon asks rhetorically: "Do they suppose that this is repeated so often for no reason? Do they suppose that these words fell from the Holy Spirit unawares?" (Ap IV, 107). These words clearly state the following with regard to the nature of Scripture: God the Holy Spirit is their author, He spoke words, and He spoke them willfully and consciously.

A similar expression confronts us in the last article of the Augsburg Confession. Melanchthon writes:

> If, then, bishops have the power to burden the churches with countless requirements and thus ensnare consciences, why does the divine Scripture so frequently forbid the making and keeping of human regulations? Why does it call them doctrines of the devil? Is it possible that the Holy Spirit warned against them for nothing? (AC XXVIII, 49)

The parallelism between the first and third questions in this citation is unmistakable. To say that the Holy Scripture forbids something is to say that God the Holy Spirit has spoken. Here again, the authorship of Biblical statements is attributed to the Holy Spirit. It is this factor that gives them their authority in the church.

Another explicit reference to the divine authorship of Scripture is found in the Formula of Concord. After setting forth the need for an unambiguous Christian witness in the world on the basis of passages from Acts, Galatians, Romans, and Colossians, the Formula continues:

At the same time this concerns the article of Christian liberty as well, an article which the Holy Spirit through the mouth of the holy apostle so seriously commanded the church to preserve, as we have just heard. (FC SD X, 15)

Here again, this confession is quite explicit in naming the Holy Spirit as the Biblical author, in ascribing intentionality to the Spirit, and in naming the apostle as the human instrument or "mouth" for the Holy Spirit. Again it is the divine authorship of the article on Christian liberty that underlies its authority.[30]

An important statement in the Formula's treatment of the Lord's Supper points to Jesus Christ as the divine author of Holy Writ. We read:

There is, of course, no more faithful or trustworthy interpreter of the words of Jesus Christ than the Lord Christ Himself, who best understands His words and heart and intention and is best qualified from the standpoint of wisdom and intelligence to explain them. In the institution of His last will and testament and of His abiding covenant and union, He uses no flowery language but the most appropriate, simple, indubitable, and clear words, just as He does in all the articles of faith and in the institution of other covenant-signs and signs of grace or sacraments, such as circumcision, the many kinds of sacrifice in the Old Testament, and holy Baptism. (FC SD VII, 50)

Remembering the close connection established between Jesus Christ and the Holy Spirit in Article III of the Augsburg Confession, we should not be surprised to find Christ named as the author of sections of Holy Scripture; for the Holy Spirit speaks from the Father and the Son. Of interest in the above reference is that our Lord's speaking of clear words in Scripture explicitly includes all articles of faith as well as many Old Testament institutions.

In seeking to understand the confessional understanding of the nature of Holy Scripture, attention must also be given to the concept "Word of God" in the Lutheran Confessions. "Word of God" has various emphases in the Lutheran Confessions. At times the "Word" has reference to Jesus Christ (AC III; FC SD VII, 39; FC SD VIII, 15—16). Often the "Word" is emphasized as the instrument of the Holy Spirit (for example, Ap XII, 40; Ap XXIV, 70; Ap XXVIII, 10; SA III, viii, 3; FC Ep II, 4), and in some of these references it appears that the word of preaching is meant. On other occasions "Word of God" appears to have primary reference to the Gospel. (For example, AC V, 4; AC XXVIII, 8—9; Ap IV, 67, 73; Ap VII, 3; Ap IX, 2; Ap XXIV, 69; FC SD II, 2.)

But most frequently the term "God's Word" indentifies "Holy Scripture." In the Preface to the *Book of Concord*, "Word of God" appears no less than 18 times as a designation for Holy Scripture. "The divine Word" and "Holy Scripture" are used as parallel expressions in the Conclusion to Part One of the Augsburg Confession. Comparison of the Latin and German texts of the Apology also furnishes ample evidence of the parallelism of the two concepts (for example, Ap II, 4; Ap XII, 16, 131; Ap XIII, 2; Ap XXI, 10; Ap XXIII, 4). "God's Word" can be read (FC SD II, 57); everything in "God's Word" is *written* for us (FC SD XI, 12); Luther's doctrine is "drawn from and conformed to the Word of God" (FC SD V, 1).

True, for some people the term "Word of God" as a designation for Holy Scripture does not necessarily mean that God is the author of the Scriptures. For the Lutheran Confessions, however, God is their author. A study of confessional contexts in which "Word of God" designates Holy Scripture suggests very strongly that the term denotes both divine authorship and authority. Reference is made to "God's Word" to establish a doctrine, condemn a false practice, give God's prescriptions for man's life, in short, to speak authoritatively. Whether reference is made to all Scripture, a particular statement of Scripture, or a message grounded on Scripture, the concept "Word of God" has reference to "a distinct word out of God's mouth, contained and preserved in the Bible."[31] If one wants to know what God has spoken or what He wills, then he must go to the Scriptures, for "we can affirm nothing about the will of God without the Word of God" (Ap XV, 17). Fagerberg's conclusion is completely in accord with the evidence:

> Whenever God's Word is mentioned, it stands in one relation-
> ship or another to the Bible. Apart from this relationship, one
> would have to decide for oneself between what goes back to God

Himself and what originates in the mouth of man .... They [the Confessions] look upon God's Word as revealed truth, found in the Bible. Inasmuch as it alone can impart the knowledge about God's will, Scripture, individual words in the Bible, or other words closely related thereto are called *God's* Word.[32]

Another confessional concept that clearly indicates the divine character of Holy Scripture is "command of God." In the confessions this term stands in close connection with the Scriptures. The first place we encounter this concept in the confessions is in the Augsburg Confession, where it is stated that "we must do all such good works as God has commanded" (AC VI, 1). The second part of the Augsburg Confession frequently uses the concept "command of God," and it is always directly or indirectly associated with a concrete Biblical statement. Holy Communion is to be distributed under both forms, the bread and wine, and the confessions refer to Matt. 26:27 as a "command of the Lord" for support (AC XXII, 1). Clerical celibacy is rejected on the basis of specific Bible passages (1 Cor. 7:2, 9; Matt. 19:11; Gen. 1:27). Then follow these words, "no law of man and no vow can nullify a commandment of God and an institution of God" (AC XXVII, 18). Such examples could be multiplied. The point is that the confessional appeal to God's command is an appeal to Holy Scripture; the concept "command of God" represents a direct or indirect connection with a specific Biblical statement."[33] Again this concept indicates that for the Lutheran Confessions Holy Scripture is *God* speaking.

Similarly the expression "divine right" is closely associated in the Lutheran Confessions with the Holy Scriptures. For something to have "divine right" it must be commanded or instituted by God; in other words, it must be based on what God says in Holy Scripture. Holy absolution, for example is "by divine right" but the enumeration of all sins is not, for it does not rest on a divine command (Ap XII, 11; see also 104 and 116). Earlier, in the development of this argument, the German text of the Apology clarifies what it means to say that something is not commanded by God, when it asserts that the opponents should have proved "out of the Holy Scriptures, out of God's Word ... that such enumeration of sins has been commanded by God" (Ap XI, 7). Holy absolution, which is nothing else than the promise of the forgiveness of sins" (Ap XII, 61), is found throughout the Scriptures and therefore exists by divine right.

Likewise, marrriage exists by divine right (Ap XXIII, 3, 6) and the law of celibacy clashes with divine and natural law. Why? Because of the clear words of Scripture that establish the divine institution of marriage, as demonstrated in the remainder of the article. Again, the distinction of hierarchical ranks in the ministry is not to be found in the Holy Scriptures, and therefore does not exist by divine right (Tr, 10). Luther maintains that "The pope is not the head of all Christendom by divine right or according to God's Word" (SA II, iv, 1).[34] When the Treatise offers to "show from the Gospel that the Roman bishop is not by divine right above all other bishops and pastors" (Tr, 7), it is clear from the context that the word "Gospel" has reference to Luke 22:24-27 and perhaps to other New Testament citations that follow. In short, by its grounding of the divine law in the words of Holy Scripture, the confessions again give evidence of their profound conviction that the words of Holy Scripture are the words of God Himself.

The accent on the divine authorship of Holy Scripture, which characterizes the Lutheran Confessions, in no way minimizes the fact that the Bible was written by men living at different times and employing different languages. The confessions frequently cite the Scriptures by referring to the human author of a passage or book. The consistent use of the principles of literary exegesis, as we shall demonstrate in Chapters 6 and 7, indicates how obvious it was for the confessors that they were dealing with flesh and blood documents in their Biblical interpretation. In fact, it is the historical human form of the Scriptures that necessitates the use of such principles. But it is important to remember that for the confessions the human authors of Holy Writ functioned instrumentally for the primary author of Scripture, God Himself. They are the "mouth" of the Holy Spirit.[35]

The confessions, to be sure, do not deal with the divine inspiration of Holy Scripture reflectively, abstractly, or philosophically, but reflect their implicit doctrine of inspiration "in an existential and functional way, without the use of philosophically refined technical terms."[36] But the Scriptures are divine revelation (SA III, i, 3). "Thus far God has revealed the mystery of foreknowledge to us in his Word" (FC SD XI, 43), even as He has revealed throughout the Scriptures what is necessary for us to know and believe. For the Lutheran Symbols, the form of Holy Scripture is simply that it is the Word of God spoken through His holy penmen.

CHAPTER 2

The Functions
of Holy Scripture

For the Lutheran Confessions the Holy Scriptures are never merely documents of the past but belong also to the present and the future. They are not only documents in which God spoke to His people thousands of years ago but books in which God addresses men today; they are *Deus loquens* as well as *Deus locutus*. In Holy Scripture God speaks directly to the reader. One is struck by the frequency with which the confessions apply passages directly to contemporaneous situations often without a discussion of the original purpose or context of the passage.

Emperor Charles V is implored not to "agree to the violent counsels of our opponents but to find other honorable ways of establishing harmony" because God "honors kings with his own name and calls them gods (Ps. 82:6), 'I say, You are gods'" (Ap XXI, 44). "The Pharisees sit on Moses' seat" (Matt. 23:2) is used in support of the doctrine that "the sacraments are efficacious even if the priests who administer them are wicked men" (AC VIII). John the Baptist's preaching is applied directly (SA III, iii, 30—32). Both Acts 5:29 and Gal. 1:8 are applied to the pontiffs "who defend godless forms of worship, idolatry, and doctrines which conflict with the Gospel" (Tr, 38). "Beware of false prophets" (Matt. 7:15) and "Do not be mismated with unbelievers" (2 Cor. 6:14) are used in support of the statement that all Christians ought to "abandon and execrate the pope and his adherents as the kingdom of the Antichrist" (Tr, 41). The words "for you" in the words of institution of the Lord's Supper "are not preached to wood or stone but to you and me" (LC V, 65). Christ's words of sorrow over Jerusalem (Matt. 23:37) show that no injustice is done when the Holy Spirit does not illuminate a man who despises His

39

instruments (FC SD II, 58). In short, the confessions approach the Scriptures under the conviction that "everything in Scripture, as St. Paul testifies, was written *for our instruction* that by steadfastness and by the encouragement of the Scriptures we might have hope" (FC Ep XI, 16, italics added; see SD XI, 12).[1]

This Word of God, which speaks directly to the reader, continues to perform indispensable functions for the church. It serves authoritatively as the only source and norm for doctrine and life; it is a unique instrument for the work of the Holy Spirit in bringing man to a knowledge of his salvation in Jesus Christ.

Source and Norm for Doctrine and Life

The classic statements in the confessions for the authoritative role of Holy Scripture in the faith and life of the church occur in the Formula of Concord. The Epitome states:

> We believe, teach, and confess that the prophetic and apostolic writings of the Old and New Testaments are the only rule and norm according to which all doctrines and teachers alike must be appraised and judged, as it is written in Ps. 119:105, "Thy Word is a lamp to my feet and a light to my path." And St. Paul says in Gal. 1:8, "Even if an angel from heaven should preach to you a gospel contrary to that which we preached to you, let him be accursed." (FC Ep Rule and Norm, 1)

The corresponding paragraph in the Solid Declaration reads:

> We pledge ourselves to the prophetic and apostolic writings of the Old and New Testaments as the pure and clear fountain of Israel, which is the only true norm according to which all teachers and teachings are to be judged and evaluated. (FC SD Rule and Norm, 3)

The contexts of both statements reinforce the sole authority of Holy Scripture. Other writings "should not be put on a par with Holy Scripture" but "should be subordinated to the Scriptures" (Ep, 2). The distinction between Holy Scripture and other writings must be maintained so that "Holy Scripture remains the only judge, rule, and norm according to which as the only touchstone all doctrines should and must be understood and judged as good or evil, right or wrong" (Ep, 7).[2] The Solid Declaration accepts Luther's judgment that the "Word of God is and should remain the sole rule and norm of all doctrine, and that no human being's writings dare be put on a par with it, but that everything must be subjected to it" (SD, 9). The Holy Scriptures, as God's product, are here sharply contrasted to merely human writings.

Taken together, these statements emphasize that Scripture is both source and norm. That Scripture is the source of doctrine is most clearly seen in the description of Holy Writ as the "fountain of Israel." This expression must be understood in the light of the meaning of "fountain" in literary contexts. Peter Fraenkel explains, "The sixteenth century, like its ancient models and ourselves, used *fons* as a technical term for literary origins or intellectual and spiritual presuppositions."[3] In the Formula, "fountain" refers to the former, that is, to the literary origin of evangelical doctrine, Holy Scripture, which is thereby described as the only valid source or basis for doctrines in the true Israel, the church of Jesus Christ.

Holy Scripture as a "norm" is still more explicit in these statements of the Formula. Substantively, the Scriptures are described as "rule" "norm" "judge" and "touchstone." Verbally, the normative function of Scripture is expressed as "judging" and "evaluating" doctrines and teachers. In short, the Formula's view of Scripture is that this divine Book has a unique position in the church. Not only is it the origin of church faith and life, but the final court of appeal for determining whether doctrines are "good or evil, right or wrong" (Ep Rule and Norm, 7).

Nor should the word "only" be overlooked in these statements. It occurs no less than four times in the descriptions of the normative function of Scripture. Not only is Scripture *a* source and norm for the church's doctrine, but it is the *only* one. The authority of Scripture is not only historically superior, not only of primary significance, but sole and absolute. The "only" is particularly striking in view of the fact that not many years previously the Council of Trent had explicitly declared that Scripture shared the normative function in the Roman Church with tradition. Fagerberg comments:

> In that situation the Evangelicals made more precise their concept of the Scriptures as the highest authority, which they derived from the reformers. It is possible that they did this also

for the purpose of repulsing long-standing traditionalist tendencies within their own groups.[4]

The Roman tradition principle and similar thinking among some Lutherans may have furnished the historical occasion for the "only," but it also remains true that the "only" really expresses nothing new for Lutheran doctrine. In view of the nature of Holy Scripture as the unique Word of God, it follows theologically that "only" Scripture can have *divine* authority in the church for doctrine.

Fagerberg is quite correct in maintaining that the Formula's "concept of the Scriptures . . . which they derived from the reformers"was not saying anything new.[5] In our previous chapter we have called attention to the self-understanding of the confessions as expositions of Scripture. We have noted many of their appeals to Scripture as the Word of God, command of God, and basis of divine right. But perhaps nothing speaks more eloquently for the confessional understanding of Scripture as the source and norm of doctrine than the continued appeal to Scripture throughout the *Book of Concord*. Of the more than seventeen hundred Biblical citations and allusions in the confessions,[6] the great majority are presented without argumentation for the authority of the passage. This was understood! Fagerberg comments:

> If the Bible had not been the self-evident point of departure, the reformers would not have taken such pains to uphold their position on the basis of Scripture, where they sought support for all articles of significance.[7]

That the Holy Scriptures alone are authoritative in doctrine is the basis of appeal in all Lutheran Confessions. The Augsburg Confession (Preface, 8; Epilog to XXI, 2; XXI, 4, German) and the Apology (I, 2; II, 32 and 42; IV, 166; XII, 16) appeal to the Sacred Scriptures as a whole as well as to individual passages as the final authority. Luther's well-known dictum "This means that the Word of God shall establish articles of faith and no one else, not even an angel" (SA II, ii, 15) is the point of view expressed in the whole *Book of Concord*. It is understandable then that one should not obey even regularly elected bishops if they err or if they teach or command something contrary to the divine Holy Scriptures" (AC XXVIII, 28). For the most serious thing that could be said against any doctrinal point of view was that it had been set forth without the authority of the Scriptures (See Ap XII, 119).

Accordingly, practices or teachings not based on Holy Scripture are to be rejected, or at best, have no certainty; in no case can they alter or set aside God's Word. "Since God's Word and command cannot be altered by any human vows or laws, our priests and clergy have taken wives to themselves" (AC XXIII, 8); the condemnation of such clerical marriage is deplorable since "in the Holy Scriptures God commanded that marriage be held in honor"(AC XXIII, 19). How will one know if any human traditions "please God since they do not have support in God's Word" (Ap XV, 14)? Similarly,

> Neither a command nor a promise nor an example can be shown from Scripture for the invocation of saints; from this it follows that consciences cannot be sure about such invocation. Since prayer ought to come from faith, how do we know that God approves such invocation? How do we know, without proof from Scripture, that the saints hear the individual's prayers? (Ap XXI, 10)

Again, Melanchthon affirms that the Roman Catholics "have no scriptural proof or command" for applying the Mass to the souls of the dead. To do such things "without the command of God and the example of Scripture" is "an abuse of the name of God in violation of the Second Commandment" (Ap XXIV, 89).

Teachings and practices without the authority of Scripture are at best uncertain. But that which God sets forth in Scripture is sure and certain. The Fourth Commandment serves as an example of this point.

> What God commands must be much nobler than anything we ourselves may devise. And because there is no greater or better teacher to be found than God, there can also be no better teaching than His. Now, He amply teaches what we should do if we wish to perform truly good works, and by commanding them He shows that He is well pleased with them. (LC I, 113)

Luther continues that performance of the duties of the Fourth Commandment is precious and pleasing to God, "not on account of your worthiness but because it has its place within that jewel and holy treasure, the Word and commandment of God" (LC I, 117). Important to remember is that this "Word and commandment of God" is to be found in the Scripture. "Hence you have a sure text and a divine testimony that God has commanded this; concerning the other things He has commanded not a word" (LC I, 120).

Thus the statement of the Formula of Concord that the Holy Scriptures are the only rule and norm in the church is not a mere principle. It is practiced throughout the confessions both in theses and antitheses, and with reference to both doctrine and life. What gives the Scriptures this authority? The confessions would answer by affirming that Holy Scripture is God's own Word. But in this connection they would also call attention to the attributes which Scripture possesses as God's Word: It is pure, truthful, and reliable. The Formula describes the Scriptures as the "pure and clear fountain of Israel" (FC SD Rule and Norm, 3). Luther urges the reader to cling to the Fourth Commandment "so that we may not again be led astray from the pure Word of God to the lying vanities of the devil" (LC I, 121). The Preface of the *Book of Concord* speaks of "the pure doctrine of God's Word," "the pure, unadulterated Word of God," "the unalterable truth of the divine Word," the pure, infallible, and unalterable Word of God," and of the "infallible truth of the divine Word."[8] An examination of the contexts of these statements shows that they are normally used when various doctrinal errors are being discussed. Thus words like "pure," "truth," "infallible," and "unalterable," when applied to Scripture, emphasize its utter reliability and freedom from every untruth.

Because we know that "God does not lie" and that "God's Word cannot err" (LC IV, 57),[9] Luther advises: Believe the Scriptures. They will not lie to you" (LC V, 76). Luther again is quoted approvingly in the Formula of Concord: "God's Word is not false nor does it lie" (FC Ep VII, 13; see FC SD VII, 96). The Holy Scriptures provided "the certain and solid basis" for the rejection of errors by the ancient church (FC SD Rule and Norm, 17). Why can the confessions be so certain of their position? Because it is based "on the Word of God as eternal truth" (FC SD

Rule and Norm, 13). If one's teaching contradicts the Scriptures, "it would be taught that God, who is the eternal Truth, contradicts Himself" (FC SD XI, 35). In short, we are "to abide by the revealed Word which cannot and will not deceive us" (FC Ep XI, 14).

Thus the truthful, pure, and infallible Scriptures serve as the only source and norm for the church's doctrine and life. All other sources of authority, such as church, bishops, and human reason, are to be subject to it and can in no way contradict it. Not only are the actual statements of the Scriptures authoritative, but deductions or inferences drawn from Scripture also have divine authority. While the confessions rule out making *our own deductions* on the basis of our speculations (FC SD XI, 55), they uphold the legitimacy of using deductions or inferences based on Scripture, as is evident in their own practice. Faith is necessary to receive the benefits of the sacraments because the sacraments are signs of the promises, and a promise is useless unless faith accepts it, as Paul teaches in Rom. 4:16 (Ap XII, 61). An important argument for infant baptism is this: The promise of salvation applies also to little children; Christ regenerates through the means of grace administered by the church; therefore it is necessary to baptize children so that the promise of salvation might be applied to them (Ap IX, 2; see also SA III, v, 4). Several non-Eucharistic passages of the New Testament are used to prove that the Lord's Supper is intended also for those whose faith is weak (FC SD VII, 70—71); this inference is possible because the confessions understand the Lord's Supper to be a form of the Gospel (SA III, iv).

The rule "Nothing has the character of a sacrament apart from the use instituted by Christ," which is used in discussing several important issues in the doctrine of the Lord's Supper, is "derived from the words of institution" (FC SD VII, 85). The Formula accepts the Christological rule, inferred from the Scriptures, that whatever the Scriptures say Christ received in time He received according to His human nature and not according to His divine nature (FC SD VIII, 57). The doctrine of the exchange of properties in Christ (which is so crucial in the debate against the Sacramentarians) is derived from the personal union and communion of natures (FC SD VIII, 31). The Formula argues inferentially: Since there is no variation with God (James 1:17), nothing was added to or detracted from the essence and properties of the divine nature in Christ through the incarnation (FC SD VIII, 49). Finally, let us note a deduction from Scripture that is also related to the interpretation of Scripture. Because everything in the Word of God is written that we might have hope, "it is beyond all doubt" that the true understanding of God's foreknowledge will not cause or support either impenitence or despair (FC SD XI, 12).

Thus the Scriptures function as the sole authority for the church, not merely by means of using Scriptural *words and phrases* in doctrinal statements but by believing, using, and living its *message,* which is divine truth itself. The clear understanding of this function of Holy Scripture is indispensable for understanding the Biblical interpretation of the Lutheran Confessions.

Soteriological Instrument

At this point in our investigation it would be simple to conclude that Holy Scripture, the divinely inspired Word and only source and norm for the church's faith and life, functions primarily to give correct information about a host of unrelated questions. While the information it gives is correct, it must be emphasized that for the Lutheran Confessions the Scriptures function preeminently as a unique instrument for the work of the Holy Spirit in bringing man to salvation. They are more than a storehouse of divine information; they confront man dynamically with the life-and-death realities of sin and salvation. Put simply, "The Word of God . . . leads us to Christ" (FC Ep XI, 7).

Already the first pages of the *Book of Concord* evidence the conviction that the Bible has to do with man's salvation. In the Preface the confessors insist that their intention in abiding by the truth of the Augsburg Confession was that other good-hearted people would be stimulated

> to investigate the truth of the divine Word that alone gives salvation, to commit themselves to it, and for the salvation of their souls and their eternal welfare to abide by it and persist in it in a Christian way without any further disputation and dissension.

46

Again, they state how mindful they are of their obligation

over against the temporal and eternal welfare of our own selves and of the subjects that belong to us to do and to continue to do everything that is useful and profitable . . . to the propagation of that Word of his that alone brings salvation.

The confessors are aware that some persons err ingenuously against the "expressed Word of God," but pastors and theologians have a responsibility to remind such persons "of the danger to their souls and to warn them against it."[10]

Luther's understanding of the dynamic nature of the Word is evident in the confessions. In his comments on the Third Commandment, he exhorts:

Therefore you must continually keep God's Word in your heart, on your lips, and in your ears. For where the heart stands idle and the Word is not heard, the devil breaks in and does his damage before we realize it. On the other hand, when we seriously ponder the Word, hear it, and put it to use, such is its power that it never departs without fruit. It always awakens new understanding, new pleasure, and a new spirit of devotion, and it constantly cleanses the heart and its meditations. For these words are not idle or dead, but effective and living. (LC I, 100—01)

Similarly, in his Preface to the Large Catechism, Luther states:

Nothing is so effectual against the devil, the world, the flesh, and all evil thoughts as to occupy oneself with the Word of God, talk about it, and meditate on it. . . . God's Word is not like some empty tale, such as the one about Dietrich of Bern, but as St. Paul says in Rom. 1:16, it is "the power of God," indeed, the power of God which burns the devil and gives us immeasurable strength, comfort, and help. (LC Preface, 10—11)

Luther can say simply: "At whatever time God's Word is taught, preached, heard, read, or pondered, there the person, the day, and the work are sanctified by it, not on account of the external work but on account of the Word which makes us all saints" (LC I, 92).

Luther's remarks obviously refer to God's Word in a wider sense than the words of the Bible. God's Word is not only something that can be read and pondered; it is to be taught and preached. It is clear that "the Word of God which alone brings salvation," as the Preface to the *Book of Concord* describes it, thus has reference to the Scripture's saving message *in any form*. The Scriptures exercise their soteriological function when they are put to use, whether in public proclamation or private study and meditation. Not surprisingly, the confessions give voice to this dynamic understanding of the Word in a variety of ways and without any precise attempt to distinguish clearly between the Scriptures themselves and their proclamation.

That God's Word is a creative word is evident in Melanchthon's comments on Gen. 1:28, which teaches that men were created to be fruitful. This Word is still creative: "The Word of God did not form the nature of men to be fruitful only at the beginning of creation, but it still does as long as this physical nature of ours exists." Likewise, the Word of God in Gen. 1:11, "Let the earth put forth vegetation, plants yielding seed," continues to make the earth fruitful. "Because of this ordinance, the earth did not begin to bring forth plants only at the beginning, but yearly the fields are clothed as long as this universe exists" (Ap XXIII, 8).

This same understanding of the Word of God as creative is applied in the confessions to the spoken Word in Baptism, the Lord's Supper, absolution, and preaching. With regard to Baptism, Luther maintains that it is not simply natural water, but a divine, heavenly, holy, and blessed water

> all by vitue of the Word, which is a heavenly, holy Word which no one can sufficiently extol, for it contains and conveys all the fullness of God. From the Word it derives its nature as a sacrament, as St. Augustine taught, *"Accedat verbum ad elementum et fit sacramentum."* This means that when the Word is added to the element or the natural substance, it becomes a sacrament, that is, a holy, divine thing and sign. (LC IV, 17—18)

The Word that Luther has in mind is Matt. 28:19 and Mark 16:16, which are "the words upon which Baptism is founded and to which everything is related that is to be said on the subject" (LC IV, 3). Not surprisingly, Luther takes issue with Thomas and the

Dominicans as well as Scotus and the Franciscans who do not attribute the power in Baptism to the Word (SA III, v, 2—3).

This accent on the power of the Word is not only Luther's but that of the other confessors as well. The Formula argues similarly with regard to Christ's presence in the Lord's Supper, namely that it is to be ascribed only to the power of God and the Word, institution, and ordinance of Jesus Christ.

> For the truthful and almightly words of Jesus Christ which he spoke in the first institution were not only efficacious in the first Supper but they still retain their validity and efficacious power in all places where the Supper is observed according to Christ's institution and where his words are used, and the body and blood of Christ are truly present, distributed, and received by the virtue and potency of the same words which Christ spoke in the first Supper. For wherever we observe His institution and speak his words over the bread and cup and distribute the blessed bread and cup, Christ himself is still active through the spoken words by the virtue of the first institution, which he wants to be repeated. (FC SD VII, 75)

After citing Chrysostom and Luther on the efficacy of the Word, the Formula emphasizes that the words of institution are under no circumstances to be omitted in the celebration of Holy Communion (79).

Melanchthon offers much the same accent with reference to the Word of God in absolution, "which is the true voice of the Gospel." Hearing the Gospel strengthens and consoles the conscience:

> Because God truly quickens through the Word, the keys truly forgive sin before him, according to the statement (Luke 10:16), "He who hears you, hears me." Therefore we must believe the voice of the one absolving no less than we would believe a voice coming from heaven. (Ap XII, 39—40)

Similarly, the Augsburg Confession states:

> At the same time the people are carefully instructed concerning the consolation of the Word of absolution so that they may esteem absolution as a great and precious thing. It is not the voice or word of the man who speaks it, but it is the Word of God,

who forgives sin, for it is spoken in God's stead and by God's command. (AC XXV, 2—3)

Here too the forgiving Word of absolution is directly related to the Word of God in Holy Scripture.

The Word of Scripture publicly proclaimed in the preaching and teaching of the church is also God's dynamic Word. The merits of Christ are offered by the preaching of God's Word (SA II, ii, 24). The Formula expresses the general view of the confessions thus:

> All who would be saved must hear this preaching, for the preaching and the hearing of God's Word are the Holy Spirit's instrument in, with, and through which he wills to act efficaciously, to convert men to God, and to work in them both to will and to achieve. (FC SD II, 52)

The Holy Spirit works through the preaching of the Law to convince the world of sin and through the preaching of the Gospel to effect man's salvation accomplished in Jesus Christ (FC SD V, 11-13). Through the preaching of the Word, God is active in both Law and Gospel; both preacher and hearer should be certain

> that, when the Word of God is preached, pure and unalloyed according to God's command and will, and when the people diligently and earnestly listen to and meditate on it, God is certainly present with his grace and gives what man is unable by his own powers to take or to give. (FC SD II, 55)

Here again the efficacious preached Word of God derives its content from the pure written Word of God if it is to be a truly divine and dynamic Word.

The emphasis on the power of the Word as set forth above is repeated often in the confessions in general statements. The Holy Spirit is given "through the Word and the sacraments, as through instruments" (AC V, 2), or simply "through the Word of God" (AC XVIII, 3). Justification takes place "only through the Word," for "one cannot deal with God or grasp him except through the Word" (Ap IV, 67), and also "faith is conceived by the Word" (73). Moreover, it is *only* through the "external Word" that God gives His Spirit, as Luther so clearly explains (SA III, viii, 3—13). Both

Luther, the Augsburg Confession (AC V, 4), and the Formula of Concord (Ep II, 13; SD XI, 76) condemn the view that God works saving faith apart from the Word. For, as Melanchthon explains, "the Word is efficacious when it is delivered by men and . . . we should not look for another word from heaven" (Ap XXVIII, 18); "it is eternal things, the Word of God and the Holy Spirit, that work eternal life in the heart" (10).

The preceding paragraphs indicate that a strong emphasis is placed by the confessions on the oral and sacramental Word. This accent is sometimes falsely placed in antithesis to the written Word of Scripture, or at least misunderstood in its relationship to Scripture. Schlink finds that "the Gospel is the norm in Scripture" and that it is "only in the act of hearing and learning, of preaching and teaching" that we meet Scripture as the Word of God.[11] Although Schlink seeks to avoid pitting the spoken Word against the written Word, the force of his statements is to make the Gospel as address or proclamation the real authority in distinction to the written Word.

Unfortunately the confessions have not dealt *explicitly* with the question of the relationship between the written and spoken Word. The manner in which they emphasize both the authority of the written Word and the efficacy of the proclaimed and sacramental Word indicates that we are not dealing here with antitheses, however. On the basis of the confessional evidence, one is compelled to agree with Fagerberg's judgment:

> But judging on the basis of what can be seen, they do not interpret the content of the spoken Word as anything other than the Word of *Scripture*. While they do not demand a literal repetition of the written Word, the content of the preached Word is not to deviate from the Scriptures. So when the Confessions mention "the Word" they refer to the written Word as often as to the proclaimed Word.[12]

To be sure, the chief content of the Scriptures is Jesus Christ, and the central message is Law and Gospel, as we shall see in Chapter 5. It is the Gospel of Jesus Christ in all its forms that is the means of grace (see SA III, iv). But for the confessions it is axiomatic that this Gospel, no less than the Law that precedes it, is grounded in Holy Scripture.

What the confessions seek to emphasize is that the Word of Holy Scripture, with its promise of grace and forgiveness in Jesus Christ, must be used and reused. This is done in the preaching of Law and Gospel and the administration of the sacraments. It is also done in listening, reading, and meditating on its content (LC I, 91; FC SD II, 16, 57; XI, 39). Fagerberg correctly summarizes this interrelationship:

> The spoken Word does not become a critical authority to be used in opposition to the Bible, but it is God's active Word in the present, precisely because it bases itself on Holy Scripture. The words of Scripture brought to life in preaching and in the administration of the sacraments are the means by which God acts.[13]

In this interrelationship, Holy Scripture carries out its primary soteriological function.

CHAPTER 3

The Clarity
and Understandability
of Scripture

For centuries before the Reformation the Bible had been regarded as a dark and mysterious book. Only the teaching office of the church was considered competent to pass judgment on the ultimate meaning of its mysteries. It was not accidental that the Lutheran Reformation's strong accents on the *sola scriptura* principle and the soteriological use of Holy Scripture should be accompanied by an equally vigorous emphasis on the basic perspicuity and general understandability of the statements of Holy Writ. For no obscure book could perform the functions that Lutherans ascribe to Scripture. This is not to say that sinful man can comprehend the spiritual mysteries revealed in Scripture through his own investigative powers. On the contrary, hand in hand with the emphasis on the fundamental clarity of the statements of Scripture goes the assertion that no man can ever spiritually comprehend the divine truth without the Holy Spirit.

For Luther the understanding of the fundamental clarity of the statements of Scripture as well as man's need for the Holy Spirit in order to comprehend its divine truth came about through his discovery of the Christological and revelatory nature of the Scriptures and the testimony of the Scripture about itself. Accordingly he emphasized both the "external clarity" of the Biblical text and the "internal clarity" of the subject matter of Holy Scripture gained through the Holy Spirit.

In his *Bondage of the Will*, Luther explains and emphasizes the importance of both concepts. First, Luther contends that the text of Scripture is fundamentally clear. Pastors and theologians especially are able to make use of the plain words of Scripture in their ministry and in their apologetics. Just as in secular society the ruling law must be plain in order to perform its task, so also in spiritual matters the Scriptures God gave to guide His people cannot be obscure. Luther lists two pages of Bible passages to show that the external clarity of Scripture is Scripture's own teaching. To be sure, there are some difficult words and passages in Scripture, but such passages can be interpreted through clearer passages and through philological and grammatical studies. If they still remain obscure, it is because of our "own linguistic and grammatical ignorance,"[1] for obscurity lies in the mind of the reader, not in the text of Scripture. Luther argues:

> In a word: if Scripture is obscure or equivocal, why need it have been brought down to us by an act of God? Surely we have enough obscurity and uncertainty within ourselves without our obscurity and uncertainty and darkness being augmented from heaven![2]

How, in fact, could Erasmus draw up an outline of Christianity if the Scriptures were obscure to him?[3]

But Luther also stresses the importance of the "internal clarity" of Scripture. He explains:

> If you speak of internal perspicuity, the truth is that nobody who has not the Spirit of God sees a jot of what is in the Scriptures. All men have their hearts darkened, so that, even when they can discuss and quote all that is in Scripture, they do not understand or really know any of it. . . . The Spirit is needed for the understanding of all Scripture and every part of Scripture.[4]

Earlier, Luther had emphasized that the contents of Scripture are plain enough for the Christian. He writes:

> For what solemn truth can the Scriptures still be concealing, now that the seals are broken, the stone rolled away from the door of the tomb, and that greatest of all mysteries brought to light—that Christ, God's Son, became man, that God is Three in One, that Christ suffered for us, and will reign forever? Take

Christ from the Scriptures—and what more will you find in them? You see, then, that the entire content of the Scriptures has now been brought to light, even though some passages which contain unknown words remain obscure.[5]

Moreover, Luther reminds his readers that Christ has opened our understanding. When people refuse to see what God reveals in Scripture, this should not be attributed to a lack of clarity in Scripture, but to the spiritual darkness of their own hearts.[6]

It is a mistake to describe Luther's concept of the clarity of Scripture solely in terms of Scripture's external textual perspicuity or exclusively in terms of its Christocentric content made understandable by the Holy Spirit. Both must be seen as integral parts of Luther's concept. Gerhard Krause correctly states: "It is now very significant for Luther's entire conception of Biblical exegesis that he himself was not content with the dogmatic assertion of a 'clarity of Scripture' in Christ."[7] Krause maintains that Luther spoke both "of the fundamental clarity of Scripture in linguistic matters and in its overall faith message."[8]

According to Peter Fraenkel, the views of Melanchthon on the clarity of Scripture were very similar to Luther's. He writes:

Just as Melanchthon had a high regard for the Scriptures as a text and connected this closely with their saving import and force, so also he thought that both the text as such and the entire matter of the Christian faith are "clear," in the sense that God has clearly revealed these mysteries for us and thus given them to us and has not left anything to our initiative to find out. . . . This is not affected by the fact that some passages are obscure and that we may have to resort to commentaries, dictionaries, or gifted exegetes to find out what they mean. For hand in hand with the perspicuity of the document goes, as we saw, the perspicuity of its subject matter, the Law and Gospel of God, the salvation offered in Christ.[9]

Likewise Martin Chemnitz, one of the major authors of the Formula of Concord, stresses both the clarity of Scripture and the need for the "gift of interpretation" from the Holy Spirit in order to explain its contents. He writes:

It is therefore certain that the teaching of the Scripture and its salutary use does not consist in words which are not understood, but in its true meaning and understanding, as the Matt. 13 parable states: ... Many passages in Scripture are indeed set forth in plain and clear words which require no farfetched interpretation but explain themselves; to these, to use Augustine's words, the door is opened both for the learned and the unlearned.

Chemnitz points out that there are indeed many difficult places in Scripture that do not immediately yield their meaning. But because God did not want to see His church fall into errors through such difficulties, "God wanted the gift of interpretation to be present in the church." And that gift is to be used "as a tool and aid for discovering and understanding the true and sound meaning of Scripture."[10]

Thus three confessional authors, Luther, Melanchthon, and Chemnitz, are agreed in their extraconfessional writings that the statements of Holy Scripture are fundamentally clear and that the Holy Spirit is necessary for us to comprehend the spiritual meaning of its content. Let us now see how these two concepts are treated in the Lutheran Confessions.

The Fundamental Clarity of Scripture

Not surprisingly, the belief in the clarity of the statements of Scripture that we find in Luther, Melanchthon, Chemnitz, and other 16th-century reformers permeates the Lutheran Confessions. Like the confessional view on the divine form of Holy Scripture, however, the confessional concept of the clarity of Scripture is not set forth in a systematic way. It is nevertheless very much in evidence. Because the reformers acknowledged that there were some passages in Scripture that were not so clear as others, it is helpful to speak of a fundamental rather than an absolute clarity of Scripture's statements.

Perhaps the most obvious and compelling confessional evidence for the fundamental clarity of Scripture is the manner in which Scripture is cited as the basis of confessional doctrine. Again and again passages are simply quoted without any explanation. Of the copious Biblical citations in the confessions, the majority are simply direct quotations of the sacred text without interpretation or extended commentary. The inference is that these statements of Scripture are so clear that anyone who can read them can also understand what they say. At times several paragraphs in succession present the confessional argument simply by quoting passage after passage almost without comment.[11] Melanchthon occasionally becomes weary of citing so much Biblical evidence, as, for example, when he is discussing human traditons, "since it is obvious throughout the Scriptures" (Ap VII, 37). In like manner, when discussing the fact that love follows faith, he concludes: "We would cite more passages if they were not obvious to every devout reader of Scripture, and we want to avoid being lengthy in order to make our case more easily understood" (Ap XII, 83). The use of Scripture in this unadorned way in documents that at least in part were intended for a nonclerical audience argues strongly for the confessional belief in the fundamental clarity and general understandability of the text of Scripture.

But there are explicit statements on the clarity of Scripture as well. The Formula of Concord describes the prophetic and apostolic Scriptures of the Old and New Testaments as "the pure and clear fountain of Israel" (FC SD Rule and Norm, 3). The description of Scripture as "clear" (lauter) or "most plain" (limpidissimus) is an affirmation that the Bible, which serves the church as its sole rule and norm for judging all teachers and teachings, is not only "pure" or without error, but also "clear"; for an unclear source of doctrine could hardly function authoritatively as a norm of doctrine.

Melanchthon contends in the Preface to the Apology that the authors of the Roman Catholic Confutation "have condemned several articles in opposition to the clear Scripture of the Holy Spirit" (Ap Preface, 9).[12] In the matter of transferring the Lord's Supper to the dead ex opere operato, the Romanists could claim support from Gregory and the later medieval theologians, but we set against them the clearest and surest passages of Scripture" (Ap XXIV, 94). The Formula maintains that the entire Apology is "supported with clear and irrefutable testimonies from the Holy Scriptures" (FC SD Rule and Norm, 6). Again, when using examples from Scripture, it is important to interpret them "according to sure and clear passages of Scripture" (Ap XXVII, 60). Implicit in such statements, especially in the use of the superlative "clearest," is the acknowledgment that some passages in Scripture are not so clear as others. The confessions maintain, however, that their doctrine in no point is based on such passages.

In article after article, the confessions assert that their argument rests on clear passages of Scripture. Communion under both kinds should be distributed because Christ commands "with clear words" that all should drink of the cup (AC XXII, 2). Some Lutheran pastors have entered the married state, since "the Scriptures clearly assert that the estate of marriage was instituted by the Lord to avoid immorality" (AC XXIII, 3). Again, "there are clear passages of divine Scripture" that forbid the establishment of human regulations to earn God's grace or as if they were necessary for salvation (AC XXVIII, 43). The passages Melanchthon has just cited "clearly call lust sin" (Ap II, 40). The distinction between civil and spiritual righteousness "is not our invention but the clear teaching of the Scriptures" (Ap XVIII, 10). In his article on justification, Melanchthon often quotes Rom. 5:2, "Through Christ we have obtained access to God by faith." "We stress this statement so often," Melanchthon explains, "because it is so clear" (Ap IV, 314). That conversion is to be attributed to God alone is demonstrated by the Formula "from clear passages of Holy Scripture" (FC SD II, 87).

Hardly any doctrinal issue of the Reformation was more closely related to the interpretation of Biblical texts than the Lord's Supper question. In spite of the many interpretations of the words of institution to which they had been exposed, the Lutheran confessors maintain that these words too are "simple" (FC Ep VII, 42), or "simple, indubitable, and clear" (FC SD VII, 50); they teach the sacramental union "clearly" (FC Ep VII, 15); "we have a clear text in the words of Christ" (LC V, 45). And so the confessions appeal that these words must be understood only "in

58

their usual, strict, and commonly accepted meaning" (FC SD VII, 48).

It is in connection with the discussion of the Lord's Supper that the Formula of Concord gives us the most explicit statement of the confessions on the scope of Biblical clarity. We read:

> In the institution of his last will and testament and of his abiding covenant and union, he uses no flowery language but the most appropriate, simple, indubitable, and clear words just as he does in all the articles of faith and in the institution of other covenant-signs and signs of grace or sacraments, such as circumcision, the many kinds of sacrifice in the Old Testament, and holy Baptism. (FC SD VII, 50)

We note that all articles of faith, the sacraments, and Old Testament sacrifices are included within the compass of Biblical clarity. Moreover, the clarity of Scripture is clearly related to Biblical language. It is therefore not in keeping with the confessional understanding of the clarity of Scripture to limit it primarily to those passages "which display the teaching of justification by grace through faith in all its force and glory."[13] As also the earlier citations in this section indicate, the confessions claimed the authority of "clear" Scripture for many other articles and practices as well.

Understanding the Scriptures by the Holy Spirit

Because the Scriptures are fundamentally clear, the reader of the Bible will be able to understand what the words themselves say, except in some passages where the language or grammar is obscure to the reader. But understanding what the words say is not always the same as spiritually comprehending the truth which God speaks in the Scriptures. For the confessions emphasize that comprehending the Scriptures in this deeper sense means to believe their Christological message, and this is possible only by the illumination of the Holy Spirit.

Anthropological considerations are basic to this confessional accent. For the confessions hold that "all men are full of evil lust and inclinations from their mothers' wombs and are unable by nature to have true fear of God and true faith in God" (AC II, 1).

This natural condition of man "is so deep a corruption of nature that reason cannot understand it. It must be believed because of the revelation in the Scriptures" (SA III, i, 3). Not only is man without fear and faith in God, but this sin of origin is responsible for all his subsequent evil deeds "which are forbidden in the Ten Commandments, such as unbelief, false belief, idolatry, being without the fear of God, presumption, despair, blindness—in short, ignorance or disregard of God" (SA III, i, 2). We note Luther's use of "ignorance or disregard of God" as a summary description of the results of man's original sin. Melanchthon also describes natural man as "ignorant of God" (Ap II, 8, 14). He approves the ancient definition which

> not only denies the obedience of man's lower powers, but also denies that he has knowledge of God, trust in God, fear and love of God, or surely the power to produce these things. (Ap II, 23)

Thus natural man is not only "ignorant of God" but lacks the spiritual power to have true "knowledge of God" (Ap II, 23).

That is not to say that natural man cannot achieve to some extent "the righteousness of reason" (Ap IV, 22). He has "freedom to choose among the works which reason by itself can grasp" and can to some extent achieve "civil righteousness or the righteousness of works" (Ap XVIII, 4). But although man has the ability to do the outward works of the law, he does not have the "spiritual capacity for true fear of God, true faith in God, true knowledge and trust that God considers, hears, and forgives us" (Ap XVIII, 7).

Natural man simply has no spiritual ability, even the ability to understand spiritual matters. The Formula declares:

> The Scripture denies to the intellect, heart, and will of the natural man every capacity, aptitude, skill, and ability to think anything good or right in spiritual matters, to understand them, to begin them, to will them, to undertake them, to do them, to accomplish or to cooperate in them as of himself. (FC SD II, 12)

Again,

> It is our teaching, faith, and confession that in spiritual matters

man's understanding and reason are blind and that he understands nothing by his own powers, as it is written in 1 Cor. 2:14, "The unspiritual man does not receive the gifts of the Spirit of God, for they are folly to him, and he is not able to understand them" when he is examined concerning spiritual things. (FC Ep II, 2)

Thus natural man lacks both the ability to understand the terrible extent of his fallen condition and the capacity to understand his justification in Jesus Christ. He understands neither Law nor Gospel, the chief message of Holy Scripture.

Therefore it is necessary that "Christ takes the law into His own hands and explains it spiritually. . . . This directs the sinner to the law and there he really learns to know his sin, an insight that Moses could never have wrung out of him." In this way the veil is removed from the Law. The Spirit of Christ, "through the office of the law, must also convince the world of sin" (FC SD V, 10—11). This operation of the Spirit through the Law is followed by His operation through the Gospel of forgiveness of sins in Christ; in this way there is kindled in man "a spark of faith which accepts the forgiveness of sins for Christ's sake and comforts itself with the promise of the Gospel. And in this way the Holy Spirit, who works all of this, is introduced into the heart" (FC SD II, 54).

The understanding of natural man's spiritual inability and consequent need for the illumination of the Spirit in the Law and the Gospel has immediate application to Biblical interpretation. For without the Holy Spirit, natural man cannot really understand the message of the Scriptures, even though he can read its words. The Formula explains that man's reason or natural intellect

is so ignorant, blind, and perverse that when even the most gifted and the most educated people on earth read or hear the Gospel of the Son of God and promise of eternal salvation, they cannot by their own powers perceive this, comprehend it, understand it, or believe and accept it as the truth. On the contrary, the more zealously and diligently they want to comprehend these spiritual things with their reason, the less they understand or believe, and until the Holy Spirit enlightens and teaches them they consider it all mere foolishness and fables. (FC SD II, 9)

The above statement is followed by no fewer than 10 Bible passages as the Scriptural basis for this view of natural man. The Formula also contends that the prayers of the saints (for example, David and Paul) for divine instruction and illumination also indicate "that what they ask of God they cannot obtain by their own natural powers." Such prayers about our ignorance were not written, however, "so that we might become remiss and lazy in reading, hearing, and meditating on the Word of God," but rather that we should thank God "for having liberated us from the darkness of ignorance and the bondage of sin and death through his Son" (FC SD II, 15).

To be sure, "the person who is not yet converted to God and regenerated can hear and read this Word externally" because man "still has something of a free will in these external matters" (FC SD II, 53). Even so,

> Although he can direct the members of his body, can hear the Gospel and meditate on it to a certain degree, and can even talk about it, as Pharisees and hypocrites do, yet he considers it folly and cannot believe it. (FC SD II, 24)

Only the operation and power of the Holy Spirit "illuminates and converts hearts so that men believe this Word and give their assent to it" (FC SD II, 55). For

> He opens the intellect and the heart to understand the Scriptures and to heed the Word, as we read in Luke 24:45, "Then he opened their minds to understand the Scriptures." Likewise, "Lydia heard us; the Lord opened her heart to give heed to what was said by Paul" (Acts 16:14). (FC SD II, 26)

This statement is followed by one of the longest catenas of Biblical proof in the Symbols, plus a quotation from St. Augustine, after which the Formula continues: "This doctrine is founded upon the Word of God" (28).

In his remarks on infant baptism, Luther argues that the baptism of infants is pleasing to God because God has significantly blessed those who were thus baptized. One of God's most significant gifts to the baptized is the gift of Biblical interpretation. He writes: "Similarly by God's grace we have been given the power to interpret the Scriptures and to know Christ, which is impossible without the Holy Spirit" (LC IV, 49).

The interpreter of Scripture who permits himself to be guided by the Lutheran Confessions knows that God Himself must enlighten his understanding to believe what God is saying in Holy Scripture. He therefore reads the clear Scriptures of God as one who has the Spirit and expects the Spirit. He needs the Spirit, not because the Scriptures are unclear, but because his own understanding is darkened by sin. Accordingly he recognizes that not even the best of Biblical scholarship can mine the depths of God's saving Word without the Spirit's gift of interpretation.

CHAPTER 4

The Central Message of Holy Scripture

With the illumination of the Holy Spirit man understands and believes the divine message of Holy Scripture. This does not mean that he now has some supernatural capacity to solve perplexing Biblical riddles or that he can fully understand the mind of God. It does mean that through the Holy Spirit he comes to know and believe God's central message to man in the Scriptures: that all men, condemned by God's Law on account of their sin, are justified by God's grace for Christ's sake through faith. The Christian man has learned to believe that in Holy Scripture God speaks a condemnatory word (Law) and a forgiving Word (Gospel), the former for the sake of the latter. He reads the Bible as one who has been justified by grace for Christ's sake through faith; he recognizes that Jesus Christ is the center of all Scripture.

The Law-Gospel Message of Scripture

The Lutheran Confessions recognize that in Holy Scripture God speaks a word of Law and a word of Gospel, a word of condemnation and a word of forgiveness, a word of death and a word of life. And they have much to say about the necessity of keeping these messages distinct from each other. So exhaustively is this theme treated in the confessions that we can do little more than summarize it in these paragraphs.

Melanchthon's argumentation in the whole Apology is closely bound up with the distinction between the Law and the promises. First, let us note his definitional and descriptive statement of these terms. He writes:

All Scripture should be divided into these two chief doctrines, the law and the promises. In some places it presents the law. In others it presents the promise of Christ; this it does either when it promises that the Messiah will come and promises forgiveness of sins, justification, and eternal life for his sake, or when, in the New Testament, the Christ who came promises forgiveness of sins, justification, and eternal life. By "law" in this discussion we mean the commandments of the Decalogue, wherever they appear in the Scriptures. (Ap IV, 5—6)

In this statement we observe the following ideas: first, the two divisions of Scripture are not identical to the distinction between the Old and New Testament but are rather to be found throughout the Scripture; second, the Law is summarized in the Decalogue, whose prescriptions appear throughout the Bible; and third, the Gospel, or promise, is Christological throughout the Scripture and is associated with forgiveness of sins, justification, and eternal life. These ideas are basic to understanding the Law-Gospel distinction throughout the confessions.

As Melanchthon explains, the chief difference between Lutherans and Roman Catholics lay in their attitude toward Law and Gospel. "Of these two doctrines our opponents select the law and by it they seek forgiveness of sins and justification" (Ap IV, 7). Lutherans, however, believe that "we cannot justify ourselves," but are justified only by the Gospel, which "is, strictly speaking, the promise of forgiveness of sins and justification because of Christ" (Ap IV, 43). On this account, the Apology argues, Roman Catholics have misinterpreted the Scriptures, for "they quote passages about law and works but omit passages about the promises" (Ap IV, 183). The proper way of interpreting Scripture is not to omit anything but to correctly interpret both Law and Gospel. And so the Apology keeps returning to the "two chief works of God in men."

These are the two chief works of God in men, to terrify and to justify and quicken the terrified. One or the other of these works is spoken of throughout Scripture. One part is the law, which reveals, denounces, and condemns sin. The other part is the Gospel, that is, the promise of grace granted in Christ. (Ap XII, 53)

It is necessary that we "distinguish between these, as Paul says (2 Tim. 2:15). We must see what the Scriptures ascribe to the law and what they ascribe to the promises." (Ap IV, 188)

It is apparent that of these two doctrines of Scripture, preeminence is to be given to the Gospel, which is God's proper work. Isaiah

> calls it God's alien work to terrify because God's own proper work is to quicken and console. But he terrifies, he says, to make room for consolation and quickening because hearts that do not feel God's wrath in their smugness spurn consolation. In this way Scripture makes a practice of joining these two, terror and consolation. (Ap XII, 51—52)

Moreover, "the teaching of the law is certainly not intended to abolish the Gospel of Christ, the propitiator." (Ap IV, 269)

Luther's confessional writings are equally clear on the Law-Gospel content of Holy Scripture. This distinction underlies his contrast of the Ten Commandments and the Creed in the Large Catechism. Luther maintains that "the Creed is a very different teaching from the Ten Commandments. The latter teach us what we ought to do; the Creed tells what God does for us and gives to us" (LC II, 67). In the Smalcald Articles Luther describes the functions of both Law and Gospel more explicitly. The "chief function or power of the law is to make original sin manifest" (III, ii, 4); it is the "thunderbolt by means of which God with one blow destroys both open sinners and false saints" (III, iii, 2). But, Luther hastens to add,

> To this office of the law the New Testament immediately adds the consoling promise of grace in the Gospel. . . . Moreover, the Gospel offers consolation and forgiveness in more ways than one, for with God there is plenteous redemption (as Ps. 130:7 puts it) from the dreadful captivity to sin, and this comes to us through the Word, the sacraments, and the like, as we shall hear. (III, iii, 4, 8)

These accents of Luther and Melanchthon are preserved in the later Formula of Concord. In the Formula an entire article is devoted to the subject, and its introductory statement is significant.

The distinction between Law and Gospel is an especially brilliant light which serves the purpose that the Word of God may be rightly divided and the writings of the holy apostles may be explained and understood correctly. We must therefore observe this distinction with particular diligence lest we confuse the two doctrines and change the Gospel into law. This would darken the merit of Christ and rob disturbed consciences of the comfort which they would otherwise have in the holy Gospel when it is preached purely and without admixture, for by it Christians can support themselves in their greatest temptations against the terrors of the law. (FC SD V, 1)

Moreover, this distinction is no Lutheran sectarian peculiarity, for "since the beginning of the world these two proclamations have continually been set forth side by side in the church of God with the proper distinction." The patriarchs and their descendants not only knew of man's sin and corruption but comforted themselves and revived their courage with the proclamation of the woman's Seed, the Seed of Abraham, the Son of David, and the Suffering Servant (FC SD V, 23). For this reason "these two doctrines must be urged constantly and diligently in the church of God until the end of the world, but with the due distinction" (FC SD V, 24).

We have already seen how the soteriological function of Scripture is related to Law and Gospel and how the illuminating power of the Holy Spirit works through both Law and Gospel. We shall not repeat these accents here. We would note at this point, however, that the Law-Gospel distinction is not something independent of Holy Scripture[1] but rather the central message of Scripture for man's salvation. Furthermore, it is to be observed that for the confessions the Gospel is clearly the "higher Word." Schlink's observation is supported by the evidence:

All previous statements about law and Gospel and about Gospel and law would be simply unintelligible if their distinction were regarded as a dialectic in which law and Gospel are with equal stress united as *God's* Word and again separated as two *different* words of God in equally stressed antithesis. The Confessions are not interested in an antithetical dialectic as such.... The Confessions do not distinguish law and Gospel for

68

the sake of a dialectic, but to extol the Gospel and exalt it far above the law. The Gospel, however, as the liberation from the curse of the law, can be extolled only because it is a word completely different from the law.[2]

The Centrality of Justification in Holy Scripture

Since the confessions extol the Gospel above the Law, it is not surprising to find that they regard the content of the Gospel as the real center of Scripture. What is the content of the Gospel? Luther describes it simply as the offer of "consolation and forgiveness ... from the dreadful captivity of sin" (SA III, ii, 8), and Melanchthon similarly defines the Gospel as the promise of "forgiveness of sins, justification, and eternal life for his [Christ's] sake" (Ap IV, 5). In a phrase, the content of the Gospel and the center of all Scripture is the doctrine of justification "by grace for Christ's sake, through faith" (AC IV). Our purpose at this point is not to give a systematic explanation of this confessional doctrine but rather to demonstrate how the Lutheran Symbols treat its relationship to Holy Scripture.

First, we note the accent on the doctrine of justification in the confessions. In the Augsburg Confession, the article on justification (IV) is the central article; the prior articles lead up to it, and those that follow it either express the consequences of justification for the faith and life of the church, or further explain the article. Of the 28 articles in the Augsburg Confession, more than half are explicitly related to the doctrine of justification.[3] Of the nearly 190 pages in the Apology, the explicit treatment of justification takes up over 60 pages; in nearly every other article, the doctrine of justification is also the obvious concern. In his Smalcald Articles Luther deals with justification explicitly in two articles (SA II, i; III, xiii), but again it is his constant concern in nearly every other topic he deals with. In fact, the Smalcald Articles are more clearly structured around the doctrine of justification than any other confessional document. Also the Formula of Concord deals extensively with this doctrine, devoting the entire third article to it. In short, the Lutheran Confessions are from beginning to end an exposition of this doctrine and a confession of it before men and God. As Herbert Bouman has stated,

A serious student of the symbols is overwhelmed by the subject. On nearly every page he meets the *cantus firmus* of justification as the ever-recurring theme which, though developed in a hundred fascinating variations, always remains plainly recognizable as the same theme.[4]

The doctrine of justification is not only the main subject of the Lutheran Confessions but the chief teaching of Scripture as well. The Augsburg Confession argues that "the chief article of the Gospel must be maintained, namely, that we obtain the grace of God through faith in Christ without our merits" (AC XXVIII, 52). Or again, "One must pay attention to the chief article of Christian doctrine, and this is not abrogated by the decree" of the apostles to abstain from blood (AC XXVIII, 66). For the Apology the doctrine of justification is "the main doctrine of Christianity" (Ap IV, 2). Melanchthon begs the emperor "to hear us out patiently and to consider carefully this most important issue, involving the chief doctrine of the Gospel, the true knowledge of Christ, and the true worship of God" (Ap XII, 3). A few lines later he repeats, "Yet the issue at hand is a great one, the chief doctrine of the Gospel, the forgiveness of sins" (Ap XII, 10).

Luther expresses himself on the article of justification with his characteristic vigor.

Nothing in this article can be given up or compromised, even if heaven and earth and things temporal should be destroyed. . . . On this article rests all that we teach and practice against the pope, the devil, and the world. Therefore we must be quite certain and have no doubts about it. Otherwise all is lost, and the pope, the devil, and all our adversaries will gain the victory. (SA II, i, 5)

Luther continues by illustrating that several Roman Catholic practices oppose the doctrine of justification by grace. The Roman Mass "runs into direct and violent conflict with this fundamental article" (SA II, ii, 1). Purgatory is "contrary to the fundamental article that Christ alone, and not the work of man, can help souls" (SA II, ii, 12). Fraternities and indulgences are "contrary to the first article" (SA II, ii, 21, 24) as are also the invocation of saints and chapters and monasteries (SA II, ii, 24;

iii, 1, 2). In fact, "all things that the pope has undertaken and done ... come into conflict with the first, fundamental article which is concerned with redemption in Jesus Christ" (SA II, iv, 3).

Luther underscores this emphasis on justification by grace in the Large Catechism when he emphasizes, "Toward forgiveness is directed everything that is to be preached concerning the sacraments and, in short, the entire Gospel and all the duties of Christianity" (LC II, 54). The Formula of Concord shares the viewpoint of the earlier confessions that the doctrine of justification is "'the chief article of the entire Christian doctrine,' 'without which no poor conscience can have any abiding comfort or rightly understand the riches of the grace of Christ'" (FC SD III, 6). It quotes Luther approvingly: "Where this single article remains pure, Christendom will remain pure, in beautiful harmony, and without any schisms. But where it does not remain pure, it is impossible to repel any error or heretical spirit" (FC SD III, 6). The Formula concludes its treatment of "this high and important article of justification before God, on which the salvation of our souls depends," by referring the reader to Luther's commentary on Galatians for a detailed explanation (FC SD III, 67).

It needs to be understood that the Lutheran Confessions see the doctrine of justification by grace to be the clear teaching of all of Holy Scripture and not a sectarian emphasis.[5] This is evident in the first instance if we take the confessions seriously as Biblical expositions; for wherever they speak doctrinally, they are doing so on the basis of Holy Scripture. But the evidence is more explicit. Melanchthon, for example, contends that the teaching that by faith alone we receive the forgiveness of sins for Christ's sake and "by faith alone are justified" has been set forth in the Apology "on the basis of Scriptures and arguments derived from the Scriptures" (Ap IV, 117). He is amazed that his opponents "are unmoved by the many passages in the Scriptures that clearly attribute justification to faith and specifically deny it to works." He asks: "Do they suppose that this is repeated so often for no reason? Do they suppose that these words fell from the Holy Spirit unawares?" (Ap IV, 107—08). Bible passages are used profusely throughout Melanchthon's presentation of justification. A case in point is the list of passages from Paul, John, Acts, Habakkuk, and Isaiah to demonstrate that the statement "Faith justifies" is found throughout Scripture. Melanchthon concludes this list with the statement, "But the Scripture is full of such testimonies" (Ap IV, 89—102). Likewise Luther's "fundamental article" on justification in the Smalcald Articles consists almost entirely of Bible passages (SA II, i). Fagerberg correctly states:

> As the promise is founded on Holy Scripture, one need not seek for a definite Word of promise, for it is present whenever God promises to raise up and restore oppressed and grieving consciences.[6]

Nor is the doctrine of justification by grace for Christ's sake through faith a teaching of the New Testament alone. The Old Testament, too, knows of no other way of being justified before God than through faith in the coming Christ. Melanchthon's definition of the Gospel in the Old Testament as the promise of justification for the sake of the coming Messiah makes this very clear (Ap IV, 5). He adds elsewhere that the promise of grace in Christ

> is repeated continually throughout Scripture; first it was given to Adam, later to the patriarchs, then illumined by the prophets, and finally proclaimed and revealed by Christ among the Jews and spread by the apostles throughout the world. (Ap XII, 53)

There has always been only one way of being justified before God.

> In the Old Testament as in the New, the saints had to be justified by faith in the promise of the forgiveness of sins given for Christ's sake. Since the beginning of the world, all the saints have had to believe that Christ would be the offering and the satisfaction for sin, as Is. 53:10 teaches, "When He makes Himself an offering for sin." (Ap XXIV, 55)

Melanchthon's use of Acts 10:43, "To Him all the prophets bear witness," is also instructive on this point, for it is Scripture's own testimony to the Christological content of the Old Testament. (See Ap IV, 83, 273; Ap XII, 65—71; Ap XX, 2.)

But Melanchthon also uses the passage to show that the

centrality of the doctrine of justification reflects the consensus of the church. He states:

> But here Peter cites the consensus of the church in support of our position. . . . Surely the consensus of the prophets should be interpreted as the consensus of the universal church. Neither to the pope nor to the church do we grant the authority to issue decrees contrary to the consensus of the prophets. (Ap XII, 66)

Again, Melanchthon explains: "Peter clearly cites the consensus of the prophets; the writings of the apostles attest that they believed the same thing; nor are testimonies of the Fathers lacking" (Ap XII, 73). Thus the confessions maintain that their central article is the chief article in Scripture and that it has been believed and confessed by the church of all ages.

One can speak of the centrality of the doctrine of justification by grace in the Scriptures, or one can speak simply of their Christocentricity, for the person and work of Jesus Christ is the *sine qua non* of justification. As the Formula states,

> Therefore we believe, teach, and confess that the total obedience of Christ's total person, which he rendered to his heavenly Father even to the most ignominious death of the cross, is reckoned to us as righteousness. (FC SD III, 56; see also 9, 23, and 30)

The reader of the confessions soon becomes aware of how frequently and steadfastly everything in Scripture is regarded as dealing directly or indirectly with Jesus Christ. And because of their conviction that all Scripture presents the same doctrine of justification for Christ's sake, it is not surprising that Christological interpretations are frequently given to Old Testament texts as well as New Testament passages. Dan. 4:27 is thus explained: "Daniel knew that the forgiveness of sins in the Christ was promised not only to the Israelites but to all nations. Otherwise he could not have promised the king forgiveness of sins" (Ap IV, 262). That the death of Christ is a satisfaction not only for guilt but also for eternal death is proved from Hos. 13:14 (Ap XII, 140). Passages from Isaiah 53 are used directly of Christ (Ap XX, 5; XXIV, 23; SA II, i, 2, 5). The burning of the lamb, the

73

drink offering, and the offering of flour mentioned in Num. 28:4-8 "depicted Christ and the whole worship of the New Testament" (Ap XXIV, 36). The Levitical propitiatory sacrifices are symbols of Christ's future offering (Ap XXIV, 24, 53). Old Testament passages support the doctrine of justification throughout the fourth article of the Apology. Three Old Testament texts (Ps. 8:6; 93:1 and Zech. 9:10) are cited to show that the prophets fortell that Christ, the God-man, is everywhere present to rule (FC SD VIII, 27). In short, the view of the confessions is that all Scripture testifies of Christ.

With this understanding of the centrality of the doctrine of justification by grace in Holy Scripture, we can understand the force of the statement in the German translation of the Apology, which reads:

> [The article of justification] is of especial service for the clear, correct understanding of the entire Holy Scriptures, and alone shows the right way to the unspeakable treasure and right knowledge of Christ, and alone opens the door to the entire Bible. (Ap IV, 2)[7]

These words contain an important Reformation emphasis on the understanding of Holy Scripture. To understand Holy Scripture is to know and believe the Christ of the Scriptures; to know and believe in Christ is to have the door to the Bible opened from the inside by the Holy Spirit and there to recognize its central message of justification by grace for Christ's sake through faith.

The emphases of the confessions presented in this chapter have important consequences for the interpretation of Holy Scripture. These will be developed more explicitly in Chapter 8. But already at this point it is clear that the confessions would answer the rhetorical question of Luther: "Take Christ from the Scriptures—and what more will you find in them?"[8] with an emphatic "Nothing!"

PART II

Confessional Principles of Biblical Interpretation

CHAPTER 5

Principles of Grammatical Exegesis

The Lutheran Confessions view the Holy Scriptures as a unit. Nowhere is Testament pitted against Testament, book against book, or author against author. As the previous chapters have indicated, the unity of Scripture is a unity of *message,* for throughout the Scriptures the divine Law and Gospel are set forth. It is a unity of *content,* for all of Scripture teaches the doctrine of justification by grace for Christ's sake through faith. Moreover, all Scripture is united in the *function* of making man wise unto salvation. And underlying the unity of message, content, and function is the unity of divine *authorship,* which gives basis and meaning to the other aspects of Biblical unity. Without a clear perception of the interrelationship of these dimensions of Biblical unity, it is impossible to understand and appreciate the specific principles of confessional Biblical interpretation

But how does the reader get at the meaning of the Word of God? How does he hear what God is saying to him in His Law and Gospel? The answer is implicit in the understanding of Scripture as God's *Word,* or the understanding of the Word of God as Holy *Scriptures.* For both "Word" and "Scriptures" imply that the Bible is to be read and interpreted as a literary document. And this is, in fact, the basic confessional answer to the above questions. We hear what God is saying in His Word through grammatical or literary exegesis of the Scriptures. It is important to see how the confessors derive the meaning from the Biblical text and seek the intended sense of the text. For in so doing they are listening to God speak.

Derive the Meaning from the Text

Perhaps the cardinal emphasis of Lutheran Reformation exegesis was its insistence that the "letters" and grammar of Scripture must be understood and taken seriously before the Scriptures can be understood theologically. Torm summarizes this emphasis: "'Letter' is and remains the foundation. The way to the religious understanding of a Biblical text goes through its letters—not over or around them."[1] How seriously the confessions take the letter of Scripture is evident in many ways, first of all in their concern with the exegesis of their Roman Catholic and "enthusiastic" opponents.

The Apology's criticism of the exegesis of the Roman Catholic *Confutation* is of three kinds. First, the Romanists are selective in their use of Scripture. "They quote passages about law and works but omit passages about the promises" (IV, 183; see also IV, 107, 221, 284, 286; XII, 34).

Second, they twist and distort the Scriptures to suit their own non-Scriptural opinions. "Our opponents twist many texts because they read their own opinions into them instead of deriving the meaning from the texts themselves" (IV, 224; see also IV, 244, 253, 255, 260, 286; XII, 123; XXIV, 115). While this "eisegesis" usually takes the form of imposing a false human opinion about justification on the text of Scripture, the Romanists also read later inventions, such as canonical satisfactions or monasticism, into the Scriptures (XII, 131; XXVII, 29).

Third, their actual exegesis is careless, slovenly, illogical, and often dishonest. They add words to the text (IV, 264) or omit a word and the central thought as well (IV, 357). They quote passages in a garbled form (IV, 286) or out of context (XXIV, 15). They are guilty of bad grammar (by applying a universal particle to a single part, IV, 283), of neglecting grammar (XII, 163), or even of despising grammar (XII, 106). Their use of logic in understanding the text is sophistic or wrong (IV, 222, 335, 360—61). They "make the effect the cause" (XX, 13). Melanchthon laments: "Who ever taught these asses such logic? This is not logic or even sophistry, but sheer dishonesty" (XII, 123). Such "exegesis" had indeed obscured "important teachings of the Scriptures and the

Fathers" (II, 32). In short, the Romanists "do violence not only to Scripture but also to the very usage of the language" (IV, 357).[2]

Like Roman Catholic exegetes, the Enthusiasts also failed to derive God's meaning from the text of Scripture itself.[3] For they "dream that the Holy Spirit does not come through the Word but because of their own preparations" (Ap XIII, 13). Luther answers this claim of the Enthusiasts in the Smalcald Articles. There he emphasizes that God gives no one His Spirit or grace "except through or with the external Word which comes before." If we maintain this truth, Luther contends, we shall be protected from those "who boast that they possess the Spirit without and before the Word and who therefore judge, interpret, and twist the Scriptures or spoken Word according to their pleasure." That Luther here condemns those who disparage the need for the external means of grace is clear. But it is also obvious that Enthusiasm includes the attempt to claim divine authority for ideas not taught in the Scriptures, for the Scriptures serve as the only source and norm for the content of the means of grace as well as for all other divine teachings. Luther's citation of the papacy as a prime example of Enthusiasm makes this plain.

> The papacy, too, is nothing but enthusiasm, for the pope boasts that "all laws are in the shrine of his heart," and he claims that whatever he decides and commands in his churches is spirit and law, even when it is above and contrary to the Scriptures or spoken Word.

Adam and Eve were Enthusiasts because they departed from the external Word of God to their own imaginations. In fact, Enthusiasm is "the source, strength, and power of all heresy, including that of the papacy and Mohammedanism" (SA III, viii, 3—13).[4]

The actual exegesis in the confessions makes it clear how seriously they took the principle of deriving the meaning from the text of Scripture. Statements like the following are frequent: "We shall simply present Paul's meaning" (Ap IV, 231); "the text does not say this" (Ap IV, 264); "as the narrative in the text shows" (Ap IV, 267); "what we have said is what Paul really and truly means" (Ap XII, 84); "where does Scripture say this?" (Ap XII, 138); "the prophet's own words give us his meaning" (Ap XXIV, 32). The appeal throughout is to what God is actually saying through His holy penmen.

The confessions evidence a careful concern for many of the aspects of grammatical exegesis. They know the importance of word study and usage. We note how carefully the words "to be justified" and "justification" are explained (Ap IV, 72).[5] Particular attention is given to understanding "faith in the true sense, as the Scriptures use the word" (Ap IV, 112; see IV, 304). Similar attention is given to deriving the meaning of the word "Gospel" from the Biblical usage, and it is noted that "the word 'Gospel' is not used in a single sense in Holy Scripture" (FC Ep V, 6; see SD V, 3—6). The Biblical meaning of the word "necessity" is studied (FC SD IV, 14, 17), and the Biblical usage of the word repentance" is analyzed (FC SD V, 7—8).

Sometimes extra-Biblical data are helpful for understanding a word used in Scripture. Commenting on the meaning of "sin offering" in Is. 53:10 and Rom. 8:3, Melanchthon comments:

> We can understand the meaning of the word more readily if we look at the customs which the heathen adopted from their misinterpretation of the patriarchal tradition. The Latins offered a sacrificial victim to placate the wrath of God when, amid great calamities, it seemed to be unusually severe; this they called a trespass offering. Sometimes they offered up human sacrifices, perhaps because they had heard that a human victim was going to placate God for the whole human race. The Greeks called them either "refuse" or "offscouring" (Ap XXIV, 23).

Later in the same article, Melanchthon discusses the use of the word "liturgy" by the Greeks. He quotes Demosthenes, the rescript of Pertinax, and Ulpian, a commentator on Demosthenes, and concludes:

> But further proofs are unnecessary since anyone who reads the Greek authors can find examples everywhere of their use of "liturgy" to mean public duties or ministrations. Because of the diphthong, philologists do not derive it from *lite,* which means prayers, but from *leita,* which means public goods; thus the verb means to care for or to administer public goods (Ap XXIV, 81—83).

Readers of the Large Catechism will also remember that Luther explains the Greek and Latin background of the word "Kirche" (LC II, 48).[6]

Particular weight is often laid on one word in a passage. The word "all" in Luke 11:41 must be clearly understood (Ap IV, 281—83). Melanchthon carefully explains the force of the word "judge" in 1 Cor. 11:31 (Ap XII, 163). The word "bread" in 1 Cor. 11:28 and 10:16 is enough Biblical basis to oppose transubstantiation (SA III, vi, 5). Much importance is attached to the exclusive particles ("alone," freely," "not of works," "it is a gift") in passages dealing with justification (Ap IV, 73; FC SD III, 52). Melanchthon feels no compulsion to do so but offers a distinction between the words "faith" and "hope" (Ap IV, 312). The Greek text is appealed to for a deeper understanding of key words. "In the Greek this petition reads, 'Deliver or keep us from the Evil One, or the Wicked One'" (LC III, 113). The Formula explains that the Greek expression "does not receive" in 1 Cor. 2:14 actually means "does not grasp, take hold of, or apprehend" (FC SD II, 12).

Grammar is of the utmost importance, as the general exegesis of the confessions from beginning to end makes very clear. The Treatise, for example, can argue that the plural form of the word "you" in Matt. 16:15, 18:18, and John 20:23 shows that the keys were given equally to all the apostles and "that all the apostles were sent out as equals" (Tr, 23).

The literary context and historical setting must also be carefully considered. Luke 7:47 is interpreted on the basis of its context, especially verse 50 (Ap IV, 152). 1 Peter 4:8 is explained on the basis of its closer context and its wider context, 2:4, 5, and 6 (Ap IV, 238). James 2:24 is explained on the basis of its context, especially 1:18 (Ap IV, 244—47). Tobit 4:11 is interpreted by verses 5 and 19 (Ap IV, 277—80). 1 Tim. 5:8, 9, and 14 help us to understand verses 11 and 12 (Ap XXVII, 64—67). That the word "Gospel" in Mark 1:1 is to be interpreted in the wider sense is based on Mark 1:4 (FC SD V, 4). Not only the context of the words of institution but also the circumstances of the Last Supper help us to understand our Lord's words of institution (FC SD VII, 44, 48). The "purpose and context of St. Paul's entire discourse" in 1 Cor. 10:18-33 help us to explain his words in verse 16 (FC SD VII,

81

57). Such examples could be multiplied. Confessional exegesis practices what Melanchthon preaches:

> It is necessary to consider passages in their context, because according to the common rule it is improper in an argument to judge or reply to a single passage without taking the whole law into account. When passages are considered in their own context, they often yield their own interpretation (Ap IV, 280).

Through careful textual study, attention to the rules of grammar and logical discourse, study of word meaning and usage, and consideration of the closer and wider context of a passage, confessional exegesis seeks to avoid the exegetical blunders of the opponents. The theological basis of careful exegesis is the conviction that God is speaking in the words of Scripture. What He is saying can be learned only by deriving the meaning of the text from the text itself.

Seek the Intended Sense of the Text

The insistence of the Lutheran Reformation that every passage of Holy Scripture has but one sense, which the exegete must discover and explain, constituted a major breakthrough in the history of Biblical interpretation.[7] In medieval times Scripture was expounded by means of the Quadriga, or fourfold rule, according to which Bible passages could have a literal, moral, allegorical, and anagogical sense. The moral or tropological sense applied to the individual believer, the allegorical to the church, and the anagogical to the future. This type of exegesis made of the Scriptures a "waxen nose," a book filled with obscurity and mystery that only the church could interpret. Farrar states:

> He [Luther] saw as clearly as Melanchthon that the pretense of a *multiplex intelligentia* destroyed the whole meaning of Scripture and deprived it of any *certain* sense at all, while it left room for the most extravagant perversions, and became a subtle method for transferring to human fallibility what belonged exclusively to the domain of revelation.[8]

It should be observed, however, that throughout the Middle Ages and into the period of the Reformation only the literal sense was valid in disputations and the exegete was not compelled to search for all four senses in every verse.[9]

Over against this view of Scripture Luther asserted: "The literal sense of Scripture alone is the whole essence of faith and Christian theology"; and again, "If we wish to handle Scripture aright, our sole effort will be to obtain the one, simple, seminal, and certain sense."[10] Or again, "The Holy Spirit is the plainest writer and speaker in heaven and earth and therefore His words cannot have more than one, and that the very simplest sense, which we call the literal, ordinary, natural sense."[11]

In his *De elementis rhetorices,* Melanchthon also disparages the fourfold sense and insists that the Scriptures have but one certain and simple sense. He writes:

> I felt that these things should be said here about the four meanings, to indicate that in each passage a single meaning, both simple and certain, is to be sought that agrees with the whole context of the statement and with the circumstances of the matter. One is not allowed to look for allegories everywhere, nor should one rashly draw something else from the grammatical statement, but one should see what fits in each place, and nothing is to be established that conflicts with articles of faith.[12]

Melanchthon explains that the one simple and certain sense is to be found by the application of the rules of grammar, rhetoric, and dialetics.[13] He adds that transforming the simple meaning of Scripture into other meanings leaves us with no certainty of Scripture's meaning and thereby weakens its authority.[14]

Once again, this principle of confessional hermeneutics can be seen most clearly in the consistent exegetical practice of setting forth the simple, literal, or native sense intended by the author as the meaning of passages. A few examples may serve to illustrate this fact. We note Melanchthon's disregard for allegories: "Our opponents will really achieve something if we let them defeat us with allegories, but it is evident that allegory does not prove or establish anything" (Ap XXIV, 35). Melanchthon ridicules such an example of Roman exegesis. Commenting on the Roman use of Prov. 27:23, "Know well the condition of your flocks," to justify a priest's investigating the sins of a penitent, Melanchthon observes:

> By a marvelous transformation, our opponents make passages of Scripture mean whatever they want them to mean. According to their interpretation, "know" here means to hear confessions, "condition" means the secrets of conscience and not outward conduct, and "flocks" means men. The interpretation surely is a neat one, worthy of these men who despise grammar (Ap XII, 106).

Melanchthon counters by pointing out that Solomon is not talking about confession but merely giving a bit of domestic advice to the head of a household. He does not, however, rule out the possibility of applying this passage to a contemporary pastor "by analogy." Again, commenting on the *Confutation's* use of 1 Sam. 2:36 to justify distributing only the bread to the laity, Melanchthon comments: "Our opponents are obviously clowning when they apply the story of Eli's sons to the sacrament" (Ap XXII, 10).

Nowhere is the confessional appeal to the native sense of the text more evident than in their interpretation of the Eucharistic words of institution. In the Large Catechism Luther emphasized: "Here we shall take our stand and see who dares to instruct Christ and alter what he has spoken. . . . For as we have it from the lips of Christ, so it is; he cannot lie or deceive" (V, 13—14). Again, "Mark this and remember it well. For upon these words rest our whole argument, protection, and defense against all errors and deceptions that have ever arisen or may yet arise" (V, 19).

The Formula of Concord deals with the interpretation of these words at great length. Because of its hermeneutical importance we shall cite the Formula in some detail. After setting forth the Sacramentarian position, the Formula quotes at length from earlier Lutheran confessions and the writings of Luther to indicate the true Lutheran position on the Real Presence. Commenting on the Wittenberg Concord of 1536, the Formula remarks:

> Thereby they wished to indicate that, even though they also use

these different formulas, "in the bread, under the bread, with the bread," they still accept the words of Christ in their strict sense and as they read, and they do not consider that in the proposition (that is, the words of Christ's testament), "This is my body," we have to do with a figurative predication, but with an unusual one (that is, it is not to be understood as a figurative, flowery formula or quibble about words). (SD VII, 38)

The Formula asserts that the Lutheran position set forth above

rests on a unique, firm, immovable, and indubitable rock of truth in the words of institution recorded in the holy Word of God and so understood, taught, and transmitted by the holy evangelists and apostles, and by their disciples and hearers in turn. (SD VII, 42)

The article then turns to an interpretation of Christ's words, pointing out that Christ speaks not as a mere man or angel, but as the one who is "himself the eternal truth and wisdom and the almighty God" (SD VII, 43). Noting the great care and deliberation with which our Lord chose His words "as he was about to begin his bitter passion and death for our sin," the Formula concludes:

We are therefore bound to interpret and explain these words of the eternal, truthful, and almighty Son of God, Jesus Christ, our Lord, Creator, and Redeemer, not as flowery, figurative, or metaphorical expressions, as they appear to our reason, but we must accept them in simple faith and due obedience in their strict and clear sense, just as they read. Nor dare we permit any objection or human contradiction, spun out of human reason, to turn us away from these words, no matter how appealing our reason may find it. (SD VII, 45)

The article cites the example of Abraham as one who did not ask for a "tolerable and loose interpretation" of God's command to sacrifice his son Isaac but "understood the words and command of God plainly and simply, as the words read" (SD VII, 46). Then it returns to the words of institution.

All circumstances of the institution of this Supper testify that these words of our Lord and Saviour Jesus Christ, which in themselves are simple, clear, manifest, certain, and indubitable, can and should be understood only in their usual, strict, and commonly accepted meaning (SD VII, 48).[15]

The next paragraphs show how the context of the Last Supper indicates that there can be no metaphor or metonymy in Christ's words. We must remain with the simple meaning of the words.

In the institution of his last will and testament and of his abiding covenant and union, he used no flowery language but the most appropriate, simple, indubitable, and clear words, just as he does in all the articles of faith and in the institution of other covenant-signs and signs of grace or sacraments, such as circumcision, the many kinds of sacrifice in the Old Testament, and holy Baptism. And so that no misunderstanding could creep in, he explained things more clearly by adding the words, "given for you, shed for you." He let his disciples keep this simple and strict understanding and commanded them to teach all nations to observe all that he had commanded them (that is, the apostles). (SD VII 50—51)

After several paragraphs dealing with further explanations of the doctrine of the Lord's Supper, the article returns to the matter of interpretation.

We shall not, can not, and should not permit any clever human opinions, no matter what appearance or prestige they may have, to lead us away from the simple, explicit, and clear understanding of Christ's word and testament to a strange meaning different from the way the letters read, but, as stated above, we shall understand and believe them in the simple sense. (SD VII, 92)

It is not surprising then that the Formula explicitly condemns those who hold that the words of institution "through tropes or a figurative interpretation are to be given a different, new, and strange sense" (SD VII, 113).

The proper sense of a passage, however, is the sense intended by the author, and the Biblical authors do not always speak in literalistic terms. This fact is also evident in the confessions. The Scriptures can employ figures of speech, for example, synecdoche (Ap IV, 152) or perhaps hyperbole (Ap IV, 277). In the same article we quoted above, the Formula asserts that John 6:48-58 refers to a "spiritual" eating of the flesh of Christ (SD VII, 61). In the following article, the Formula adopts Luther's explanation that the right hand of God "is not a specific place in heaven, as the Sacramentarians maintain without proof from the Holy Scriptures. The right hand of God is precisely the almighty power of God which fills heaven and earth . . ." (SD VIII, 28). Our Lord's statement in Matt. 16:18, "On this rock I will build my church," does not have reference to a literal rock, but to the ministry of the confession which Peter made when he declared Jesus to be the Christ, the Son of God" (Tr 25).[16]

The confessions throughout give evidence of their diligence in seeking the intended sense of the text. Their refusal to indicate several meanings for any passage shows how faithfully they carried out their further conviction that each passage has but one single sense. But are there exceptions to this last principle? Some would find exceptions in Luther's treatment of three commandments and in Melanchthon's interpretation of Levitical sacrifices. With regard to the Third Commandment, Luther writes:

> Therefore, according to its literal, outward sense this commandment does not concern us Christians. It is an entirely external matter, like the other ordinances of the Old Testament connected with particular customs, persons, times, and places, from all of which we are now set free through Christ. (LC I, 82)

Luther then proceeds to offer "ordinary people a Christian interpretation of what God requires in this commandment" (LC I, 83). At first glance it would appear that Luther interprets the Third Commandment as having a double sense, the one "literal" and the other "Christian." But as Luther's context makes clear, the true and proper sense of the commandment is its "Christian" sense, and it was also this for the Old Testament Jews. Its proper sense, then and now, is "That we should sanctify the holy day or day of rest" (LC I, 81). True, "As far as outward observance is concerned, the commandment was given to the Jews alone" (LC I, 80), but this "outward observance" for Luther is not the real, proper meaning of the text. Much the same explanation should be given to Luther's remarks on the last two commandments:

"These two commandments, taken literally, were given exclusively to the Jews; nevertheless, in part they also apply to us" (LC I, 293).[17]

A related problem greets us in Melanchthon's comments on the Levitical sacrifices in Article XXIV of the Apology. All Levitical sacrifices can be classified under two heads, propitiatory or eucharistic (21). Yet, there has really been only one propitiatory sacrifice in the world, the death of Christ (22). What then were the Levitical "propitiatory" sacrifices? They "were so called only as symbols of a future offering" (24). That is, "they were merely a picture of the sacrifice of Christ which was to be the one propitiatory sacrifice" (53). However, "by analogy they were satisfactions since they gained the righteousness of the ceremonial law and prevented the exclusion of the sinner from the commonwealth" (14).[18] For the Apology there is but one proper meaning of the Levitical "propitiatory" sacrifices: They are symbols of the coming sacrifice of Christ. The New Testament (in this case, the book of Hebrews) has not added another meaning to their original meaning. In fact, it is only by way of "similitude" to what they signify that they are called "propitiatory" in terms of their civil function in the Israelite community.

Thus the confessional conviction that Holy Scripture is the clear literary Word of God is demonstrated in their continual practice of careful and sober grammatical exegesis. In their literary interpretation of Scripture the confessional authors use every tool at their disposal to derive the one intended meaning of the text from the text itself. For the confessions, excellency of scholarly exegesis was not an option but a theological necessity. For God's message to man does not lie behind or above or apart from the Word, but in the Word of Scripture. Any other approach to the message of Scripture is Enthusiasm.

CHAPTER 6

Let Scripture Interpret Itself

The principles of grammatical exegesis noted in the last chapter, while grounded ultimately in the literary nature of Holy Scripture as God's Word, are generally applicable to the interpretation of any piece of literature. In a sense it is also true that any document must be permitted to interpret itself. But in the breadth and intensity of its application, the principle of the self-interpreting Scripture can only be understood theologically. For the Bible is in reality a collection of 66 different documents written in different times and cultures by many different men. That the Bible can interpret itself is a legitimate principle of interpretation for the Lutheran Confessions only because of the *unity* of Scripture, which is a unity of authorship, content, and purpose, and because of its fundamental *clarity*. After looking briefly at the historical background of this interpretative principle, let us observe it in practice in the confessions, first with regard to individual passages of Scripture and then with articles of faith derived from Scripture.

Historical Background

The classic formulation "Holy Scripture is its own interpreter" is evident in Luther's writings as early as 1519 and continued to play an important role in his Biblical exposition.[1] Karl Holl calls attention to the significance of this emphasis of Luther's:

Luther rejects the claim that the churchly authority raised for itself with respect to the right of Scripture interpretation. But even more important was the positive emphasis lying within it, namely, the priority given the inherent rights of an original source. Accordingly, Luther's emphasis was an event for the whole intellectual discipline.[2]

The Lutheran Reformation gave this principle classic expression and meaning. And yet it cannot be said to be a new discovery of Luther's since many of his predecessors also employed it.[3] It is not surprising that some observers regard Luther's emphasis on the clarity and self-interpreting nature of the Scriptures to have been motivated primarily by his desire to free Scripture from the need of ecclesiastical interpretation.[4] That this principle did indeed help to accomplish this cannot be denied. Moreover, it helped place the Book of Life into the hands of anyone who could read and stimulated exegetes to search the Scriptures. But that this principle was more a historical necessity than a theological deduction for the Reformers cannot be granted. For it follows not only from the revelatory nature of the Word but from its unity of divine authorship, content, and purpose.

Prior to the writing of the Lutheran Confessions in the *Book of Concord,* the principle that Scripture is to interpret itself had been set forth confessionally in *The Ansbach Evangelical Counsel* of 1524. Not only does the *Counsel* emphasize the distinction between men's word and God's Word, but it also points out that one should explain "writing with writing and one text of the Bible through or with another."[5] An earlier statement emphasized that no passage in Scripture "can be in conflict with another, and the divine Scripture can be discerned at all locations."[6] An entire article is devoted to the clarity of the Scriptures. Here it is pointed out that Scripture is "in itself and by its nature understandable" because the Holy Ghost has spoken clearly and understandably and still speaks in His own writing."[7] Article 41, entitled "Resolution on the Interpretation of Scripture", emphasizes two things: that Scripture is only "interpreted through the Spirit of God" and that the divine Scriptures must be interpreted through one text with another."[8] Although the methodology of interpreting Scripture set forth in the *Counsel* has been called "Biblicistic,"[9] the fact remains that in emphasizing the principle of the self-interpreting Scripture this document was simply giving expression to an idea that was taught and practiced by Luther and the other reformers.

Applied to Individual Passages

In the practice of exegesis the principle "Holy Scripture is its own interpreter" means that passages dealing with the same subject matter may be used to explain or corroborate each other. More importantly, and this has been its chief use in Lutheran circles, the principle means that the less clear or plain passages are to be considered in the light of the clearer ones. Figurative or metaphorical expressions, for example, may be clarified by passages that speak on the same subject in plain and simple language. Fagerberg summarizes the function of this principle in confessional exegesis thus:

> In principle, the meaning of Scripture is clear, and what it intends to say can be formulated in comprehensive statements. When there is some doubt about the meaning of a given passage, such a passage must be understood in the light of those whose meaning is clear.[10]

The principle of the self-interpreting Scripture is consistently followed in the confessions. It is in evidence in the many places where long lists of passages are cited as being in agreement with each other and therefore expressing the same truth. A few examples will illustrate this. Passages from Paul and John are used side by side (Ap IV, 29—33), as are citations from Paul, John, Acts, Habbakuk, and Isaiah (Ap IV, 88—89). 1 Corinthians, Ephesians, Matthew, Acts, John, and Colossians are cited in the same paragraph (FC SD II, 10). In one paragraph of the Formula, 15 different Biblical books are cited (FC SD II, 26). Passages from Romans, Genesis, and Hebrews are cited together to explain how Abraham was justified before God through faith alone (FC SD III, 33). The mutually explanatory nature of Scripture passages is further evidenced by the use, without comment or explanation, of Old Testament passages with reference to New Testament Christians. For example, Old Testament passages are used to describe the voluntary nature of the works done by the "people of the New Testament" (FC SD IV, 17). A passage from Deut. 12 is used as the

91

basis of the assertion that believers should not "set up a self-elected service of God without his Word and command" (FC SD VI, 20).

Often a passage is cited simply to corroborate the interpretation given to another passage. Thus the meaning of "remembrance" in 1 Cor. 11:24 is illustrated by the citation of Ps. 111:4,5 (Ap XXIV, 72). That Matt. 26:27 indicates that *all* communicants should receive the sacramental wine is reinforced by the evidence of 1 Cor. 11:20-34 (AC XXII, 2—3). The Formula cites 1 Cor. 10:16-21 to show that the words of institution teach the real presence of Christ's body and blood in the Lord's Supper (FC SD VII, 54-60).

Moreover, the hermeneutical principle that Scripture should interpret itself is stated rather explicitly in the confessions. In his article on monastic vows, Melanchthon deals with the Roman Catholic interpretation of the vows of the Nazarites and Rechabites. He states:

> Besides, examples ought to be interpreted according to the rule, that is, according to sure and clear passages of Scripture, not against the rule or the passages. It is a sure thing that our observances do not merit the forgiveness of sins or justification. When the Rechabites are praised, therefore, we must note that they did not observe their way of life out of the belief that they would merit forgiveness of sins by it. (Ap XXVII, 60—61)

It is to be noted that Melanchton's use of the doctrine of justification to clarify the nature of Rechabite vows is an application of the rule that sure and clear Scripture passages interpret those that are unclear; he is not here using justification by grace as an independent hermeneutical principle. Melanchthon has much the same point in mind when he says with reference to Luke 11:41 ("Give alms; and behold, everything is clean for you"): "A study of the whole passage shows its agreement with the rest of Scripture" (Ap IV, 284).

The principle that Scripture is to interpret itself is particularly helpful in finding the meaning of a passage that is somewhat obscure or difficult to interpret. Of key significance for understanding the interpretation of the Law in the Apology are the following statements:

In the preaching of the law there are two things we must always keep in mind. First, we cannot keep the law unless we have been reborn by faith in Christ, as Christ says (John 15:5), "Apart from me you can do nothing." Secondly, though men can at most do certain outward works, this universal statement must be permitted to interpret the entire law (Heb. 11:6), "Without faith it is impossible to please God" (Ap IV, 256).

Whenever law and works are mentioned, we must know that Christ, the mediator, should not be excluded. He is the end of the law (Rom. 10:4), and he himself says, "Apart from me you can do nothing" (John 15:5). By this rule, as we have said earlier, all passages on works can be interpreted (Ap IV, 372).

We should note at this point that the Apology's "rule," without which neither the Law nor works can be understood, again consists of clear passages of Holy Scripture. The further significance of this "rule" will be discussed in the next chapter.

Other examples of the confessional use of this principle to clarify passages should be noted. That Paul in Rom. 3:28 is talking about the whole law, and not just Levitical ceremonies, is proved not only from Rom. 7:7 and 4:1-6 but also from Eph. 2:8 (Ap IV, 87). The scope of Matt. 23:3 ("Observe whatever they tell you") is limited by Acts 5:29 ("We must obey God rather than men") (Ap XXVIII, 21). The plural form of "you" in John 20:23 (as well as in two Matthean passages) indicates that in Matt. 16:15 Christ was addressing not only Peter, but Peter as representative of the entire company of apostles (Tr, 23). Luke 24:46-47, a passage which does not contain the word "Gospel," is used to explain the word "Gospel" in Mark 16:15 (FC SD V, 4). The reason that some of those who receive the Word with joy fall away again (Luke 8:13) is not that "God does not want to impart the grace of perseverance to those in whom he has 'begun the good work.' This would contradict St. Paul in Phil. 1:6" (FC SD XI, 42). The Second Commandment, which enjoins the proper use of God's name, explains "the question that has tormented so many teachers: why swearing is forbidden in the Gospel [Matt. 5:33—37]. and yet Christ, St. Paul [Matt. 26:63-64; Gal. 1:20; 2 Cor. 1:23] and other saints took oaths" (LC I, 65). Proverbs 10:12 helps us to understand 1 Peter 4:8, "Love covers a multitude of sins" (Ap IV, 238—40).

Of particular interest is the confessional use of New Testament passages to interpret Old Testament ones. Eph. 5:9 and Col. 3:10 are used to interpret "image of God" in Gen. 1:27 (Ap II, 18, 20). Abraham's faith and Abel's sacrifice are explained on the basis of Rom. 4:9-22 and Hebrews 11:4 (Ap IV, 202). "Purify yourselves, you who bear the vessels of the Lord" (Is. 52:11) is interpreted by Titus 1:15, "To the pure all things are pure" (Ap XXIII, 64). The Levitical sacrifices are interpreted as symbolical of Christ's death on the basis of the Epistle to the Hebrews (Ap XXIV, 20, 22, 53). That the drink offering referred to in Num. 28:4-8 has reference to the sanctifying of believers throughout the world with the blood of Christ is proved by 1 Peter 1:2 (Ap XXIV, 36). In an extremely interesting use of Scripture, the Formula cites Gen. 17:4-8, 19-21, against the Anabaptist denial of infant baptism (SD XII, 13 and Ep XII, 8). Paul's words in Rom. 8:7 and Gal. 5:17 explain Gen. 8:21, "The imagination of man's heart is evil from his youth" (FC SD II, 17).

And so the confessions continually draw from all parts of Scripture to corroborate, explain, or interpret passages in any other part. Yet this is not done capriciously. In the Leipzig Debate of 1519 Luther observed that it is not the "right way to interpret Scripture, to collect statements from different parts of the Bible without any regard for logical order or context."[11] The confessions are mindful of this advice, for their use of other passages to explain a concept or statement is attempted with a conscious regard for logical order, content, and context.

Applied to Articles of Faith

Not only do the confessions use individual passages of Holy Scripture to explain other passages, but they also make use of entire articles of faith in evaluating a passage or the interpretation that has been given to a passage. This is particularly true with regard to the doctrine of justification by grace, but it is also true of other articles. In reality, however, this is not another principle of interpretation but an extension of the rule that

Scripture is its own interpreter. For the confessions understand their articles of faith to be drawn from the Scriptures.[12]

We see this principle in operation in the first article of the Formula of Concord. Over against the contention of Flacius that original sin is man's substance, the Formula argues that a distinction must be made between our nature as it was created by God and the original sin that dwells in the nature and corrupts it. Why? "Because the chief articles of our Christian faith constrain and compel us to maintain such a distinction" (FC SD I, 34). The article goes on to show how the articles of creation, redemption, sanctification, and resurrection are opposed to the Flacian position. The article of creation teaches "that even after the Fall God is man's creator who creates body and soul for him." To identify corrupted man with sin itself would be to make God "the creator of sin" (38). The article of redemption teaches "that God's Son assumed our nature, though without sin." The Flacian position would compel one to hold "that Christ either did not assume our nature inasmuch as he did not assume sin, or that Christ assumed sin inasmuch as he assumed our nature" (43—44). The article of sanctification teaches "that God cleanses man from sin"; the Flacian position cannot be correct, because God receives man into his grace . . . but remains the enemy of sin throughout eternity!" (45). The doctrine of the resurrection teaches that our flesh and soul will be raised to be with God, yet without sin; Flacius' position would force us to hold either that in the resurrection we will have another soul and body or that "sin would be raised and would be and remain in the elect in eternal life" (46—47). It must be understood that Flacius, too, based his view on Bible passages. Thus the argumentation of the Formula from articles of faith has reference to Flacius' Biblical interpretation of passages dealing with sin.

That "articles of faith" in the above paragraphs are nothing other than the teaching of Holy Scripture on the four topics cited is evident from the parallel statements: "According to the Holy Scriptures we must and can consider, discuss, and believe these two as distinct from each other" (FC SD I, 33), and "The chief articles of our Christian faith constrain and compel us to make such a distinction" (FC SD I, 34). Furthermore, in each of the four articles the Formula either explicitly demonstrates or claims a Scriptural basis. In its explanation of the article of creation, the Formula cites no fewer than 10 passages from Scripture as the basis of the article (34—42). In the article of redemption, "we have the mighty testimony of Scripture"; both alternatives posed by the Flacian position "are contrary to the Scriptures" (43—44). In the article of sanctification "we have the testimony of Scripture" (45) and in the doctrine of the resurrection "Scripture testifies" to the correct understanding (46). Thus it is evident that the Formula's use of "articles of faith" in evaluating Flacius' position is in reality a broad, and important, application of the principle that Scripture interprets Scripture.

Much the same principle is evidenced when the confessions interpret passages or argue from the basis of the doctrine of justification by grace, as they do often, especially in the Apology. For example, in discussing the phrase, "love, which is the bond of perfection" in Col. 3:14, Melanchthon says that Paul is obviously discussing love for the neighbor, for "Paul would never permit Christ, the propitiator, to be excluded, and hence this view is far removed from his intention" (Ap IV, 231). Later in the same article he urges us to keep the important teaching of the Gospel in view in order to understand the preaching of penitence (Ap IV, 260). Melanchthon prefers to call Tobit 4:11, "Alms free from every sin and death," a hyperbole "so as not to take away from the glory of Christ" (Ap IV, 277). The Apology rejects the notion that there must be sacrifices in the New Testament besides the death of Christ that are valid for the sins of others because

> This notion completely negates the merit of Christ's suffering and the righteousness of faith, it corrupts the teaching of both the Old and the New Testament, and it replaces Christ as our mediator and propitiator with priests and sacrificers who daily peddle their wares in the churches. (Ap XXIV, 57)

Similarly we note the rejection of the idea that the Mass benefits *ex opere operato* because it conflicts with the righteousness of faith (Ap XXIV, 60). Pelagians and others who deny that original sin is sin are condemned, "for they hold that natural man is made righteous by his own powers, thus disparaging the sufferings and merit of Christ" (AC II, 3). Earlier we have noted how Luther rejects a number of Roman Catholic practices because of their opposition to this fundamental article.[13]

The hermeneutical significance of the article of justification will be discussed more completely in the following chapter, but already here we wish to emphasize that the use of the chief article of faith in the manner evidenced in the previous paragraph is an application of the principle "Holy Scripture is its own interpreter." This is evident, first, from Melanchthon's description of the content of this principle as "the sure and clear passages of Scripture" (Ap XXVII, 60). In the context of this definition, Melanchthon then describes as a "sure thing" the teaching "that our observances do not merit the forgiveness of sins or justification" (Ap XXVII, 61). The doctrine of justification is here the example of the rule, not the rule itself. Second, we have already seen that the confessions not only derive the doctrine of justification from Scripture but regard it as the very center of Scripture.[14] Even where the argument is from the doctrine of justification, the context immediately suggests that it is the *Scriptural* doctrine of justification that is meant. Since the doctrine of justification is the "fundamental article" of the Scriptures of the Old and New Testaments, it is not surprising that its use as an important aspect of the principle of the self-interpreting Scripture should be so frequent in the Lutheran Confessions.

The principle that Scripture is to interpret Scripture, whether individual passages or entire articles are employed, is a theological principle of literary exegesis. Its validity and reliability rests ultimately on the Biblical unity of authorship, content, and purpose. The fact that the Scriptures were authored by God the Holy Spirit suggests that this principle is ultimately an extension of the general hermeneutical principle of literary exegesis that any passage must be considered and explained in terms of its context. Thus the context of any Bible passage is the entire Scripture, since all Scripture is authored by the same Holy Spirit. That the "context" of Scripture can give a *true* explanation of any passage rests on the fact of its *divine* authorship, by virtue of which Scripture is held to be in agreement with itself. For as we have seen, the confessions regard the "Word of God as the eternal truth" (FC SD Rule and Norm, 13); they believe that "God's Word cannot err" (LC IV, 57); they do not believe that God, "who is the eternal Truth, contradicts himself" (FC SD XI, 35). Moreover, the Christological content and soteriological purpose of all Scripture suggest that Biblical materials in various parts of the Scripture and in various literary forms can be used together, for they ultimately speak of the same Christ and seek to bring to man the same salvation by grace.

CHAPTER 7

The Hermeneutical Function of Law-Gospel and Justification

The confessional commitment to careful grammatical exegesis and the use of the principle of the self-interpreting Scripture are largely grounded theologically in the divine authorship of Holy Scripture. We have also observed that the confessions emphasize that Law and Gospel are the basic message of Holy Scripture, that justification by grace for Christ's sake through faith is the center of all Scripture, and that the primary function of Holy Scripture is to make man wise unto salvation. This chapter is an attempt to determine what role the understanding of the soteriological content and purpose of Holy Scripture plays in confessional hermeneutics.

Not General Hermeneutical Principles

With its insistence that all of Holy Scripture "should be divided into these two chief doctrines, the law and the promises" (Ap IV, 5) and its never-ending refrain that justification by grace is the fundamental article of all Scripture, it is not surprising that some should feel that here we have the most important hermeneutical principles for a Lutheran understanding of Holy Scripture. Edmund Schlink, who speaks for a large number of Lutheran theologians, emphasizes not only the hermeneutical significance of the Law-Gospel distinction but also that the Gospel is the basic norm in the Scripture and that Scripture is normative only for the sake of the Gospel.[1] A document distributed in 1965 to clergy members of The Lutheran Church—Missouri Synod and the American Lutheran Church for study and discussion emphasizes the importance of the doctrine of justification for Biblical interpretation. The document makes some very strong claims for the interpretative significance of this doctrine. It maintains that "all theology that receives its dimensions and contours from this guiding principle is pure and true." It states:

> The doctrine of the forgiveness of sins through faith in Christ is not only the *praecipuus locus doctrinae christianae* ("main doctrine of Christianity"), but it also determines the interpretation of all Scripture.

Again, "Where this soteriological concern is present, exegesis, whether it deals with a single article of faith or with Scripture as a whole, will lead to basically the same application." Because of its almost complete silence on any other hermeneutical directives, the document gives the impression that for the Lutheran Confessions the doctrine of justification is the overarching hermeneutical principle.[2]

But can this position be maintained on the basis of the confessions themselves? Those who would answer affirmatively often cite the following confessional passages:

> The distinction between law and Gospel is an especially brilliant light which serves the purpose that the Word of God may be rightly divided and the writings of the holy prophets and apostles may be explained and understood correctly (FC SD V, 1).

> [The article of justification] is of especial service for the clear, correct understanding of the entire Holy Scriptures, and alone shows the way to the unspeakable treasure and right knowledge of Christ, and alone opens the door to the entire Bible... (Ap IV, 2, German).[3]

The citation from the Formula quite obviously describes a basic Lutheran perspective or presupposition for explaining and understanding the Scriptures. But what does it mean to distinguish Law and Gospel? The immediate context answers: that we do not "confuse the two doctrines and change the Gospel into law." Confusing the doctrines of Law and Gospel means that "what belongs to one doctrine is ascribed to the other"; thus "the two doctrines would be tangled together and made into one doctrine" (FC SD V, 27). In effect, the Formula is saying: What is Law in Scripture must be explained and understood as Law, and what is Gospel in Scripture must be explained and understood as Gospel. If all Scripture is understood and explained as Law there will be no instrument for the Spirit to create faith in Christ and as a result no comfort against the terrors of the Law. If all Scripture is explained and understood as Gospel, there will be no instrument for the Spirit to convict man of his sin and show him his need for a Savior, thereby weakening also the force of the Gospel. But the citation from the Formula does not answer these questions directly: How do I determine whether a passage in Scripture is Law or Gospel or both? When I have determined whether it is Law or Gospel, how do I derive the specific Law message or specific Gospel message from the passage?[4] The Formula, judging from its own methodology, would answer: through the illumination of the Holy Spirit in the practice of careful grammatical exegesis. This passage does *not* suggest that the distinction between Law and Gospel is a general hermeneutical principle to be applied to every text of Scripture in order to discover its meaning.

The citation from the German translation of the Apology likewise expresses a most important Lutheran consideration for understanding the Scriptures. For to have a clear and correct "understanding of the entire Holy Scriptures" is to know and believe their central message of salvation in Jesus Christ. To have the door opened "to the entire Bible" means to read the Bible with the illumination of the Spirit and as a believing Christian, knowing that in it and through it God speaks to us about our Savior and through His Spirit makes us His sons! In short, the German Apology is here expressing the conviction of the confessions that the Scriptures are Christocentric and that their central purpose is to make men wise unto salvation. The man who believes the doctrine of justification by grace will understand this; he will see that everything in the Bible is directly or indirectly related to this center. As one who knows himself to be justified by God's grace he will expect and find nothing in the divine Scriptures to be contrary to this doctrine; he will have his eyes opened by the Spirit to the wonders of God's grace throughout the Scriptures. Moreover, this understanding of justification will help him understand what the Scriptures say about the relationship of faith and works.

If the Law-Gospel distinction and the doctrine of justification by grace were hermeneutical principles of general applicability, or even the dominant hermeneutical principles, it is difficult to understand why the confessions bring nonsoteriological questions to the Scriptures for an answer, or answer them from the Scriptures without the explicit help of such soteriological hermeneutical principles. For the questions of whether both bread and wine are to be administered to the laity in the Lord's Supper and the questions about clerical celibacy, monastic life, obedience to civil government, and the descent to hell are all treated by the confessions without explicit appeal to soteriological principles. On the other hand, emphasis on the doctrine of justification as a general and dominant hermeneutical principle could be understood to mean that the confessions impose this doctrine on texts of Scripture where it does not in fact occur. This, as we have seen, is not the case, for the confessions not only derive the doctrine of justification from the Scriptures, but insist on the general necessity of deriving the meaning from the texts themselves (Ap IV, 224). Moreover, it must be remembered that the chief issue for much of the confessions is the interpretation of the Gospel itself. What *is* the Gospel according to Scripture? To suggest that the Gospel served as a hermeneutical principle for answering this question is begging the question. As Fagerberg observes, "One can find no basic limitation to questions directly connected with the distinction between Law and Gospel." [5]

But the most accurate answer to this question can come only through observing the actual exegesis of the confessions. Let us look at the exegesis of a passage where the doctrine of justification is clearly the issue: the interpretation of James 2:24, "You see that a man is justified by works and not by faith alone" (Ap IV, 244—53). The Apology reaches the conclusion that this passage does not violate the Pauline doctrine of justification by grace, not by imposing Paul's teaching *upon* the James passage but by deriving it *from* the passage through careful grammatical exegesis. The Apology is interested in "what James meant" (244). It carefully reads the text, noting that James "does not omit faith nor exalt love in preference to it" (245). It takes the context seriously by pointing out that in James 1:18 "regeneration takes place through the Gospel" (247). Thus, "the context demonstrates that the works spoken of here are those that follow faith" (246). In short, "James says none of this, which our opponents shamelessly infer from his words" (253). Nowhere in the whole chain of argumentation is a Law-Gospel hermeneutical principle applied, nor is there any evidence that the confessions considered this an "obscure" passage requiring interpretation by a clearer one. James *teaches*—he is not *made* to teach—justification by grace.

Similarly, 1 Peter 4:8, "Love covers a multitude of sins," is explained on the basis of the context (1 Peter 2:4, 5, 6), which clearly teaches the necessity of being built on Christ; the Old Testament background (Prov. 2:10); and a parallel passage (Col. 3:13). The doctrine of justification enters into the interpretation, but not artificially (Ap IV, 238—41). In explaining Col. 3:14, "love, which is the bond of perfection," Melanchthon says, "we shall simply present Paul's meaning" (Ap IV, 231—37), which has to do with fellowship in the church rather than personal perfection. Again, the doctrine of justification is present in Melanchthon's argumentation, but not in such a way that it determines the meaning of the text.

If we turn our attention to the confessional interpretation of passages in which the doctrine of justification was not the issue, we find no evidence that the Law-Gospel distinction or the doctrine of justification functioned as hermeneutical principles in such instances. For example, in the Formula's lengthy discussion of one of the most controverted passages in the 16th century, "This is my body,"[6] the appeal is consistently made to deriving the meaning from the text itself, using the context and setting of the Last Supper, and noting parallel passages. Neither the doctrine of justification nor the Law-Gospel distinction are brought to bear on the passage.

103

Another very controversial question was the issue of papal supremacy. The Roman Catholics attempted to defend their position on the basis of passages like Matt. 16:18, "You are Peter, and on this rock I will build my church," and Matt. 16:19, "I will give you the keys." Melanchthon contends that these words were not spoken to Peter alone, but to Peter as the representative of the entire company of apostles. His reasons are given: (1) The context explains that Jesus was talking to all disciples because in Matt. 16:15 Jesus used the plural form of "you" and Matt. 18:19 shows that the keys were given to the church rather than to a particular person; (2) parallel passages, such as John 20:23 and Matt. 18:18, speak in the plural rather than the singular; (3) the article of faith that the ministry is valid only because of the Word given by Christ; and (4) "most of the holy Fathers" agree with Melanchthon's interpretation. Nowhere in the interpretation is there evidence of the Law-Gospel distinction or the principle of justification being used to explain the passage (Tr, 22—29).

In short, the confessions themselves do not support the notion that the Law-Gospel distinction or the doctrine of justification serve as an overarching hermeneutical principle of general applicability to the Scriptures. With regard to "the rule concerning Law and Gospel," Fagerberg states: "The rule was never applied as an obtrusive hermeneutic principle, and least of all set over the Scriptures as an authority."[7] With regard to the doctrine of justification he contends:

> ... justification is important because of its basis in Scripture, and it makes good sense of what Scripture says about salvation. But this doctrine is not a general key to the Scriptures. Instead of being the sole principle for the interpretation of the Scriptures, it provides the basic rule which clarifies the Scriptural view concerning the relation between faith and good works.[8]

In a similar way, Gerhard Gloege, while emphasizing the hermeneutical significance of the doctrine of justification for the Reformers, concludes:

> This does not mean that the doctrine of justification functions as a hermeneutical "principle" in the sense that with its help every possible text of the Old or New Testament can speak of

justification, that is, be expounded or applied with reference to justification. On the contrary![9]

In fact, had the confessions employed the doctrine of justification in this way, their exegesis would have been just as open to the charge of subjectivism as was that of their Roman Catholic and Enthusiast opponents.

Clarifying Passages Dealing with Faith and Works

To state that the doctrine of justification and the Law-Gospel distinction are not hermeneutical principles of general applicability does not imply that they serve no hermeneutical function for confessional exegesis. In our last chapter we called attention to the use of the article of justification by grace as an aspect of the principle that Scripture interprets itself.[10] There it was noted that the doctrine of justification is drawn from Scripture and that Law and Gospel are the message of Scripture. It should be further noted that whenever the confessions appeal to either the Law-Gospel distinction or the doctrine of justification in the interpretation of a passage, this always occurs with passages or practices where the doctrine of justification is at stake or where the proper distinction between Law and Gospel may be blurred. In this sense we can speak of the Law-Gospel distinction and the doctrine of justification as hermeneutical principles. *In such passages* the Law-Gospel distinction and the doctrine of justification function as applications of the hermeneutical principle that Scripture must interpret itself. In short, the Lutheran Confessions use the Law-Gospel distinction and the doctrine of justification as hermeneutical principles in clarifying the Biblical data dealing with the relationship between faith and works. Because *all* Scripture is divided into Law and Gospel and *all* Scripture testifies to the same doctrine of justification, it is not surprising that the use of these doctrines as hermeneutical principles should be so frequent in the confessions.

Fagerberg explains that Law and Gospel "is a means of guidance for Bible readers in those sometimes confusing areas where statements are made about good works, and give all of these passages a uniform meaning." He points out that Law and

Gospel therefore have much to say about the proper understanding of the Christian life.[11] Similarly, the doctrine of justification functions as "the basic rule which clarifies the Scriptural view concerning the relation between faith and good works." The primary intentions of Melanchthon in the Apology, according to Fagerberg, were to illustrate that the Lutheran doctrine of justification is Scriptural and to explain how apparently contradictory statements of Holy Scripture with reference to Christian good works are to be understood. In performing this last function, the doctrine of justification "makes good sense of what Scripture says about salvation."[12] In other words, the confessions use the Biblical doctrine of justification and the Biblical Law-Gospel distinction to define important Biblical principles with reference to the relationship between faith and works and the Christian life in general. Let us look at some of the more important applications.

First, the Law cannot be kept "unless we have been reborn by faith in Christ"; "this universal statement must be permitted to interpret the entire law (Heb. 11:6), 'Without faith it is impossible to please God'" (Ap IV, 256). Christ "is the end of the law (Rom. 10:4), and he himself says, 'Apart from me you can do nothing' (John 15:5). By this rule, as we have said earlier, all passages on works can be interpreted" (Ap IV, 372).

Second, good works are fruits of faith. "We must come back to the rule that without Christ the teaching of the law has no value. Thus God is pleased by that almsgiving which follows justification or reconciliation, not by that which precedes" (Ap IV, 277—78). Love is the greatest virtue, but it does not justify. Only faith in Christ justifies, and only the justified man can truly love God and neighbor (Ap IV, 224—30).

Third, the Christian is bound to do good works because God has commanded them (AC VI). Being bound to the commands of God[13] is a liberating principle, for it releases us from the obligation to follow humanly devised practices (SA II, ii, 2; Ap XXIV, 89). But good works must be done, not to gain justification, but "because God has commanded them" (Ap IV, 189; see Ap XXVII, 54). "Penitence ought to produce good fruits. What these fruits are, we learn from the commandments. . . . These fruits are commanded by God" (Ap XII, 174). Closely related is the recognition that Christian vocation is the life commanded by God.

> The Gospel does not overthrow civil authority, the state, and marriage but requires that all these be kept as true orders of God and that everyone, each according to his own calling, manifest Christian love and genuine good works in his station of life. (AC XVI, 5)

Luther's interpretation of the commandments reinforces this point. All commandments proceed from the First Commandment, which teaches the fear, love, and trust of God (LC I, 324, 326—28). The Fourth Commandment specifically gives the Christian calling its divine sanction, but all commandments are interpreted as God's will for man in his vocation.

Fourth, some Biblical prescriptions were temporary and therefore no longer obligate Christians. In the first place this applies to certain apostolic practices. Apostolic authority was limited to the Word of God; we believe them on the basis of another's Word rather than on the basis of their own"; therefore, their own traditions are not binding (Ap XXVIII, 18). The prescriptions of Acts 15 were not intended to be permanent and do not place a new yoke around the neck of the disciples. For the apostles "did not contradict their own writings," and they consistently seek to stress Christian liberty and to free the church from the idea that "human rites are necessary acts of worship" (Ap XXVIII, 16).

Closely related is the principle that only the Moral Law, and not the political and ceremonial laws of the Old Testament, bind the Christian today. The reason for this lies in Scripture itself. The prime example is the abrogation of the Sabbath law: "The Scriptures, not the church, abrogated the Sabbath, for after the revelation of the Gospel all ceremonies of the Mosaic law can be omitted" (AC XVIII, 59). Insisting that the Levitical laws about uncleanness no longer apply because the Gospel frees us from them, the Apology refers to the way in which the apostles resisted similar legalism in Acts 15 (Ap XXIII, 41—42). New Testament worship is spiritual, consisting of the righteousness of faith in the heart and the fruits of faith, and "it abrogates Levitical worship"

(Ap XXIV, 27). After a long list of Bible passages, Melanchthon continues: "Therefore, as we discern the shadow in the Old Testament, so in the New we should look for what it represents and not for another symbol that seems to be a sacrifice" (37). It was the insistent contention of the confessors that their Roman Catholic opponents failed to make this all-important distinction (Ap XV, 4, 10, 30; XVI, 3; XXIV, 52). Such a practice, Melanchthon maintains, "corrupts the teaching of both the Old and the New Testament" (Ap XXIV, 57).

It is to be observed that in enumerating these principles for understanding the relationship between faith and good works, the confessions are not merely making deductions from the Scripturally based doctrine of justification by grace, but claim explicit Scriptural basis for each. The first principle appeals to two Bible passages, but these passages merely express succinctly what the confessions find all of Scripture to be saying. The other principles, too, are elaborated on the basis of Scripture. In other words, even in passages dealing with faith and works where the doctrine of justification or the Law-Gospel distinction are used as hermeneutical principles, the confessions seek to make it clear that they are letting Scripture interpret Scripture.

General Presuppositions for Biblical Exegesis

While the doctrines of justification and Law and Gospel do not serve as overarching heremeneutical principles of general applicability, they do serve as hermeneutical principles in interpreting the Biblical data with reference to faith and works. Moreover, these doctrines serve the confessional interpreter as presuppositions for his exegetical labors throughout the Scriptures.

The Lutheran Confessions have much to say about the presuppositions of their opponents and maintain that their false presuppositions are to a large extent responsible for their faulty exegesis. The Scholastics minimize the doctrine of original sin (Ap II, 8) and emphasize man's ability to keep especially the Second Table of the Law (Ap IV, 34). They "select the law and by it they seek forgiveness of sins and justification" (Ap IV, 7). They do not really "know how the forgiveness of sins takes place" (Ap

IV, 20). When one holds that man can contribute to his salvation, the role of Jesus Christ is understandably diminished. "What need is there for the grace of Christ if we can become righteous by our own righteousness?" (Ap II, 10). Such a faulty understanding of soteriology and anthropology had its effect on the scholastic exegesis of the Scriptures. The Roman Catholic opponents interpret passages of Holy Scripture "in either a philosophical or Jewish manner" (Ap IV, 376) by making the Bible conform to the exegete's own preconceptions. They are unmoved by the many clear passages on justification by grace (Ap IV, 107); they "read their own opinions into them instead of deriving the meaning from the texts themselves" (Ap IV, 224); they "maliciously twist the Scriptures to suit the man-made theory that by our works we purchase the forgiveness of sins" (Ap IV, 260); "they quote passages about law and works but omit passages about the promises" (Ap IV, 183). The practice of this Scholastic exegesis is a clear example of how faulty soteriological presuppositions can adversely affect Biblical exegesis.

In reacting against this kind of exegesis, however, the Lutheran Confessions do not suggest another arbitrarily chosen set of presuppositions, but rather permit the Bible's own testimony to its content to provide the proper hermeneutical perspective. As we have seen, the confessions see the central message of Scripture to be the justification of the condemned sinner by grace for Christ's sake through faith.[14] And it is this Christocentric message of Scripture, seen and believed by the illumination of the Holy Spirit, that serves the Lutheran interpreter as a general presupposition for the interpretation of the entire Scripture.

This Christocentric understanding of Scripture helps the Biblical interpreter by reminding him that all Scripture is ultimately related to Christ and the justification of the sinner for His sake. This is true of the Old Testament no less than the New, for the confessions take seriously Acts 10:43: "To him all the prophets bear witness" (Ap IV, 83; Ap XII, 66, 73; Ap XX, 2).[15] In this sense the doctrine of justification serves positively to inform all Biblical interpretation and negatively to warn all interpretation that does not magnify Christ and His grace that it has

109

departed from the Scripture's own understanding of its content and purpose.

For the Scriptures are the Word that alone brings salvation."[16] As the Formula declares:

> All Scripture, inspired by God, should minister not to security and impenitence but "to reproof, correction, and improvement" (II Tim. 3:16). Furthermore, everything in the Word of God is written down for us, not for the purpose of thereby driving us to despair but in order that "by steadfastness, by the encouragement of the Scriptures we might have hope" (Rom. 15:4). (FC SD XI, 12)

Accordingly the Formula states that "any interpretation of the Scriptures which weakens or even removes this comfort and hope is contrary to the Holy Spirit's will and intent" (FC SD XI, 92). The conviction that Biblical interpretation is ultimately to bring Gospel hope, comfort, and consolation to troubled consciences is a characteristic of all confessional exegesis. One of the chief confessional complaints about Romanist exegesis is that it lacks this capacity.[17]

The Biblical interpreter who approaches the Scriptures with the soteriological presuppositions of the Lutheran Confessions will expect to hear God speak His Law and His Gospel. He will expect to have his understanding of God's saving grace in Christ deepened and strengthened. He will expect to find the same Christ whom he knows and believes as a baptized and believing Christian living by the power of the Word. All of this he will expect and find. In this anticipatory function, the doctrines of justification and Law-Gospel serve to prevent Biblical exegesis from becoming fragmentized and distorted by keeping it true to the Bible's own Christological content and soteriological purpose.

In this way the doctrine of justification by grace and the distinction between Law and Gospel are vital presuppositions for the proper interpretation of Scripture. These presuppositions, moreover, are derived from the Scriptures themselves and epitomize the content of the entire Bible. As such they serve as controls over against interpretations of Scripture that weaken the doctrine of justification by grace for Christ's sake through faith or confuse the condemning Law with the saving Gospel. As clearly taught Scripture doctrines they also function as hermeneutical principles in interpreting the Biblical data dealing with Christian faith and works. But they are not general hermeneutical principles for deriving the meaning from the text of Scripture; they are rather the central message of Holy Scripture. What God is saying in His Law and Gospel can only be heard through the ears of a Spirit-illuminated grammatical exegesis that employs principles of interpretation consonant with the nature, content, and purpose of God's Book of Life.

CHAPTER 8

The Testimony
of the Fathers
and Biblical Interpretation

The Lutheran Confessions are thoroughly grounded in Holy Scripture. Not only do they see themselves as Biblical expositions and summaries, but from beginning to end, implicitly and explicitly, they acknowledge the supreme authority of God's written Word. Even the principles of Biblical interpretation they employ are derived from the nature, content, and purpose of Holy Scripture. In their persistent application of the Christocentricity of Holy Scripture, they make it plain that *solus Christus* and *sola scriptura* are inextricably interwoven. But the *sola scriptura* principle in the Lutheran Confessions does not mean a disregard for the testimony of the fathers or the tradition of the church. In fact the confessions manifest the opposite: a grateful, yet careful and critical appreciation of the doctrinal continuity of the church. Our intention here is not to examine in depth the confessional understanding of traditon but rather to note the manner in which the confessions make use of the testimony of the fathers in their Biblical interpretation.

The intention of the Lutheran Confessions to preserve Lutheran continuity with the church of all times is evident in many different ways. It is manifest not only in the preservation of many church customs and ceremonies[1] but especially in their continued acceptance of the dogmas of the early church such as Christology and the Trinity. It was not the intention of the Reformation to be radically different or new, but to be a critical and reformed continuation of the true church of Christ.

This is evident not only in the acceptance of the ancient

ecumenical creeds in the *Book of Concord* (FC SD Rule and Norm, 4) but elsewhere. The first article of the Augsburg Confession accepts and confesses the doctrine of the Trinity "in accordance with the decree of the Council of Nicaea" (AC I, 1). Luther begins his Smalcald Articles with summary statements on the doctrines of God and Christology that explicitly name and use the language of the Apostles' and Athanasian Creeds. Article III of the Augsburg Confession employs much of the language of the Second Article of the Apostles' Creed. Heresies condemned by the ancient church are condemned by the Lutheran Confessions: Arians, Samosatenes, Manichaeans (AC I), Pelagians (AC II; FC II), Donatists (AC VIII), and Novatians (AC XII).

Moreover, the doctrinal continuity with the ancient church is evident in the frequent citation of the early fathers of the church. The list of patristic citations in the confessions fills eleven pages![2] Such citation is most in evidence when the confessions are dealing with controversial topics. With reference to the doctrine of justification, Melanchthon can claim: "We have proof for this position of ours not only in the Scriptures, but also in the Fathers" (Ap IV, 29). The Lutheran doctrine of original sin is contrary neither to Scripture nor "the church catholic," but it is an illumination of "important teachings of the Scriptures and the Fathers" (Ap II, 32). "All the Scriptures and the church" proclaim that the demands of the Law cannot be satisfied by man (Ap IV, 166). That "the whole church confesses that eternal life comes through mercy" has many clear testimonies "in the Scriptures and in the Church Fathers" (Ap IV, 322—24). Melanchthon advises: "Let no one think that we are teaching anything new in this regard when the Church Fathers have so clearly handed down the doctrine that we need mercy even in our good works" (Ap IV, 325). With regard to giving undue honor to our good works, Melanchthon states that "we could quote endless passages from Scripture and the Fathers, but we have already said enough on this subject" (Ap XX, 5). The idea that the Mass benefits *ex opere operato* is not to be found anywhere in the Fathers" (Ap XXIV, 67; see 97). The conviction that a church practice contrary to God's command should not be followed is not only derived from Scripture, but is ancient canonical teaching (AC XXII, 9).

Although patristic citations are not so frequent in Luther's confessional writings as in Melanchthon's, they are not altogether lacking. He appeals twice to St. Jerome in the matter of church government (SA II, iv, 9; III, x, 3). He refers to Bernard, Gerson, and Huss (LC IV, 50). Moreover, his rejection of uncatholic Enthusiasm and Anabaptism, as well as his acceptance of the early creeds, and his use of traditional catechetical materials in the catechisms indicate his desire to reform and continue the church rather than to build anew. Ten paragraphs of the Treatise are devoted to an analysis of evidence from the early church on the question of papal primacy (12-21). The later Formula of Concord, too, can argue that the doctrine of the real presence in the Lord's Supper has been "the unanimous teaching of the leading Church Fathers" (FC Ep VII, 15).

Not surprisingly, therefore, the Lutheran Confessions maintain their doctrinal continuity with the ancient church. Melanchthon claims: "They [our preachers] have not introduced any innovations, but have set forth the Holy Scriptures and the teachings of the holy Fathers" (Ap II, 50). The Augsburg Confession maintains, "that we have introduced nothing, either in doctrine or in ceremonies, that is contrary to Holy Scripture or the universal Christian church" (AC Conclusion, 5). It is important to take this claim seriously, for it indicates that the Lutheran Confessions do not see themselves as just another interpretation of Scripture but as *catholic* Biblical exposition. Such claims are made not only for the confessions as such but for the interpretation of individual passages as well. Melanchthon, for example, claims that his interpretation of "on this rock" in Matt. 16:18 has the support of "most of the holy Fathers" (Tr, 27-29).

But the confessional claim to be in agreement with the Fathers needs clarification, for the confessions manifest no uncritical acceptance of ecclesiastical tradition. In fact, a study of the word "tradition" in the confessions reveals that it was for them a largely negative concept. *Traditiones* and *Menschensatzungen* are virtually synonymous with "human works." For Luther, for example, "human traditions" identify those practices and teachings introduced by the church without God's Word for the purpose of meriting salvation, and he understandably con-

115

demns them (SA III, xv, 1). This kind of tradition includes such condemned practices as the enumeration of all sins in confession and the need for satisfactions following absolution (Ap XI, 6—8; Ap XII, 11, 143—45). Such traditions are closely related in principle to the Mosaic Ceremonial Law (Ap XV, 10) and are to be opposed because they contradict God's will and command in Holy Scripture (Ap XXVIII, 20). Both Luther and Melanchthon place God's Word and human traditions in antithesis, frequently citing Matt. 15:9, "In vain do they worship me, teaching as doctrines the precepts of men."[3]

This negative attitude toward human traditions indicates that the Lutheran appreciation of the testimony of the fathers is not unmixed with severe criticism and that the supreme judge of all traditions is Holy Scripture. This distinction between the Scriptures and the fathers is clearly set forth by the confessions. For the fathers "were men and they could err and be deceived"; moreover, there is also great variety among them. Rather than basing our doctrine on the fathers, Melanchthon argues, we follow "the surest and clearest passages of Scripture" (Ap XXIV, 94—95). For there are many weak people in the church who build perishing structures of stubble on the true foundation of Christ and faith. "The writings of the holy Fathers show that even they sometimes built stubble on the foundation but that this did not overthrow their faith" (Ap VII, 20—21).

Luther's comments in the Smalcald Articles are particularly instructive for understanding the confessions' critical acceptance of the fathers. Luther is not ready to accept the Roman Catholic opinion that St. Augustine taught that there is a purgatory, for Augustine mentions only that his mother had asked to be remembered at the altar. Even this, Luther maintains, "is nothing but a human opinion of certain individuals and cannot establish an article of faith. That is the prerogative of God alone." Only when the Roman Catholics have abolished their traffic in purgatorial Masses will Luther be ready to discuss with them "whether statements of St. Augustine are to be accepted when they are without the support of the Scriptures." For "it will not do to make articles of faith out of the holy Fathers' words or works.

116

... This means that the Word of God shall establish articles of faith and no one else, not even an angel" (SA II, ii, 13—15).

Other examples of this critical view of tradition are apparent. The concept of confession had undergone a change from the early church writers (Ap XII, 112). The authority of bishops had increased over the course of the years (Tr, 70—71), and the enumeration of seven sacraments is by no means universal in the fathers (Ap XIII, 2). Communion under one kind only as well as transubstantiation are of relatively recent origin (SA III, vi, 2—5; AC XXII, 4—10). The marriage of priests has support in the early church and some fathers (AC XXIII, 10—12, 18).

This variation between praise and criticism of ecclesiastical tradition follows Melanchthon's general concept of church history. For him church history follows a pattern of alternating cycles of degeneration and reformation. The truth of God at various periods of history was often nearly lost, only to be restored through reformation. During the periods of degeneration the true church has lived on as a minority church. But through all periods of its history, the church has preserved a continuity of doctrine, just as the Lutheran Reformation was preserving it in the 16th century. Thus the task of the church was not to create new doctrines but to restore to light the doctrinal truth that has always been confessed by the church, even though it may often have been a minority church.[4] This view of church history is apparent when the Augsburg Confession states that "one holy Christian church will be and remain forever" (AC VII, 1). It is evident in the assertion that the Gospel promise was first given "to Adam, later to the patriarchs, then illumined by the prophets, and finally proclaimed and revealed by Christ among the Jews, and spread by the apostles throughout the world" (Ap XII, 53). Many of the above accents are obvious in Article XII of the Apology (68—71).[5] This view of the pattern of church history helps explain both the negative and positive evaluation of the testimony of the fathers in the confessions. As Fagerberg explains:

> The truth was given and established once and for all time. Those fathers whose work was acceptable had not formulated

117

any new doctrines; they had restored the original ones and freed them from irrelevant additions. The Confessions sought to return to those fathers who had preserved the pure doctrines, without falsification.[6]

But to judge the writings of the fathers in this way requires a higher norm, and this the confessions find in the Holy Scriptures, which are "the only rule and norm according to which all doctrines and teachers alike must be appraised and judged" (FC Ep Rule and Norm, 1). Other writings of ancient and modern teachers, whatever their names, should not be put on a par with Scripture but should be received in no other way than as "witnesses to the fashion in which the doctrine of the prophets and apostles was preserved in post-apostolic times" (FC Ep Rule and Norm, 2). Any doctrine, Biblical exposition, or practice in agreement with Scripture was accepted as genuine tradition, but whatever contradicted Holy Scripture was rejected. In short, "according to the Lutheran Confessions the real basis of all legitimate tradition is nothing other than the ecclesiastical exposition of the Bible."[7]

With this understanding of the role of the testimony of the fathers in the Lutheran Confessions we are in a better position to evaluate its function for confessional Biblical interpretation. All Biblical interpretation as well as church practice must be measured by the norm of Holy Scripture. This means that certain past expositions will be found wanting or wrong and will therefore be discarded. It means that much in the history of Biblical interpretation will be found to be true and will therefore be preserved. For "what the saints in the church have believed since the beginning of the world" (Ap XII, 73) remains the same: the Gospel of Jesus Christ taught in the Scriptures of God and proclaimed from age to age.

This identity of the church's Biblically based proclamation and faith throughout all ages serves Biblical interpretation in a positive way as a guide for proper ecclesiastical exegesis. Brunstaedt explains:

The Scripture and its truth proves itself in the consensus of Biblical interpretation. The Biblical interpretation of the

118

Fathers was not an extension of the Scriptures, but rather something for us to place alongside of and under the Scriptures. The more agreement, so much less the risk of arbitrary interpretation of Scripture. The consensus is a sign of the truth of the correct Biblical interpretation.[8]

In the confessions we see this most clearly in the acceptance and use of the ancient catholic creeds, which because they are Biblical and catholic, also serve to guide the interpreter into the Scriptures. The confessions certainly do not suggest that the testimony of the fathers is a source or norm of doctrine, let alone a hermeneutical principle for Biblical interpretation. But they do suggest that the Biblical testimony of the fathers, extending from the age of Adam to the present age, can serve Biblical interpretation as a hermeneutical guide by summoning the interpreter to the task of appreciative, yet critical listening to the saints of yesterday.

CHAPTER 9

Confessional Biblical
Interpretation Today

The testimony of the fathers which agrees with Holy Scripture, particularly as it is incorporated in the ecumenical creeds, served the framers of the 16th-century Lutheran Confessions as a hermeneutical guide. For Lutherans today the Lutheran Confessions themselves serve as the genuine Biblical testimony of the fathers in much the same way. For contemporary Lutherans claim to accept the confessions as the confessions themselves wish to be understood, namely, as correct Biblical expositions. With the signers of the Formula of Concord they agree that the confessional *corpus* serves a normative function in the church "because it is drawn from the Word of God" (FC SD Rule and Norm, 10). And in precisely this function the confessions direct us to Holy Scripture as "the only rule and norm according to which all doctrines and teachers alike must be appraised and judged" (FC Ep Rule and Norm, 1).

Vilmos Vajta speaks of this "hermeneutic function" of the confessions in connection with the continuing theological and churchly task of testing all presuppositions of Scriptural interpretation. Although Scripture and the confessions are to be distinguished, they "are at the same time bound together by the hermeneutic function of the confessions." The confessional writings "provide the key to understanding the Holy Scriptures, although at the same time they are subordinate to the Scriptures and their interpretation must be repeatedly reexamined in the light of the Scriptures." Vajta emphasizes particularly the manner in which the confessions "go to the very core of the Gospel in such a way as to illuminate the Scriptures." He emphasizes that the continuous movement from the Bible to confession must be accompanied by a movement from the confession to the Bible. For the confessional "pretention to an unadulterated interpretation can only be maintained if it proves itself in continuous interpretation of the Scriptures."[1] Vajta's "hermeneutic function" of the confessions, in other words, means the impetus and direction which the confessions give to the church's ongoing study of Holy Scripture.

This "hermeneutic function" of the confessions can serve all facets of the faith and life of the contemporary church, including the important area of Biblical interpretation. To be sure, the guidance of the confessions in this or any other area will be ineffective unless the confessions are accepted as correct Biblical expositions. While there is truth in Vajta's assertion that "the individual details of exegesis in the confessional writings do not claim to be normative,"[2] it must not be forgotten that "he who unconditionally subscribes to the Symbolical Books declares that the interpretations which are contained in the Symbols are 'according to the analogy of faith.'"[3] In other words, the confessional impulse to continuous Biblical interpretation in no wise calls into question the validity of the confessions as truthful Biblical expositions. In fact, subscription to the Lutheran Confessions means that the contemporary Lutheran interpreter of the Scriptures accepts not only the conclusions of the Biblical exegesis that constitutes the doctrinal content of the confessions but also the hermeneutical principles employed by the confessions in reaching their conclusions. For, as we have seen, the confessional principles of Biblical interpretation are theologically grounded in the confessional doctrine of the Word. If the confessional testimony of the fathers is to give the contemporary church guidance also in the area of Biblical interpretation, it is important that we note some of the more important conclusions and implications of this study.

The confessional understanding of the nature, content, and function of Holy Scripture is the theological foundation of confessional Biblical interpretation. For the confessions, Holy Scripture is the divinely authored and infallible Word of God throughout which God speaks the condemnatory word of Law and the forgiving word of Gospel in order to make men wise unto salvation through faith in Christ Jesus. As God's own speech, the Scriptures have God's own authority and power, not only as the church's doctrinal and ethical norm but also as the content of God's message, which awakens men from the death of sin to the life of Christ. In Holy Scripture God has expressed Himself with clarity in all articles of faith, and yet the blindness of natural man's heart prevents him from understanding the full meaning of God's written Word without the illumination of the Holy Spirit. But with the Holy Spirit the Christian interpreter of Holy Scripture recognizes and believes the central content of all Scripture, Jesus Christ. He therefore interprets Holy Scripture as a literary and theological unit, for he knows that all Scripture has one Author, one content, and serves one primary soteriological purpose.

But the Holy Scriptures, as their name suggests, are literary documents and as such can be interpreted only through careful study of the text.⁴ The confessions evidence their serious intention of deriving the meaning from the text by a sober and consistent analysis of words, grammar, and context. They permit Scripture to interpret itself by studying parallel passages or entire articles of faith derived from the Scriptures, a procedure grounded in their conviction that Scripture is a literary and theological unit. They seek the intended sense of the text, whether the language of the text is literalistic or figurative, and they are convinced that every text of Scripture has but one meaning. Reading the Scriptures as literary documents is not an option for the confessions, for they are convinced that God's authorship of Scripture was accomplished through human authors living and writing at various times as men of their times. The confessions oppose every suggestion that God's intended meaning in Scripture lies anywhere but in the words themselves.

The confessional understanding of the Christological content and soteriological function of all Scripture gives direction and purpose to the exegetical application of their hermeneutical principles. In their grammatical exegesis, the confessions explain the Scriptures of both the Old and New Testaments from the center of all Scripture, Jesus Christ. Throughout the Scriptures they hear God speaking Law and Gospel for the gracious justification of all men through faith in Jesus Christ. Their conviction that Scripture is God's Word for man's salvation helps them avoid a purely rationalistic or informational approach to the Book of Life. But they hear God's gracious message throughout the Scriptures not through textual manipulation or imposition, but through careful and honest exegesis; for they are convinced that the message of forgiveness and life in Jesus Christ is precisely what God is saying to men of every age in the text of Holy Scripture.

Thus the confessions see and maintain an indissoluble connection between the *sola scriptura* and *solus Christus* principles. The *sola scriptura* principle ultimately has meaning only in the unfolding of Scripture's Christological content for its soteriological purpose. The *solus Christus* principle has its validity and authority only from the Holy Scriptures authored by God and used by Him to bring man to faith in Jesus Christ. Both principles depend for their understanding and acceptance upon the Holy Spirit, who is not only the Spirit of Christ and the primary Author of Holy Scripture but the Lord and Giver of life. The confessions confess the Christ of *Scripture,* even as they ground all theology on the Scripture testifying to *Christ.*

Finally, it should be noted that the confessional principles of Biblical interpretation are not a set of rules and guidelines so carefully and minutely formulated that they will yield guaranteed and unanimous results in every exegetical detail if followed consistently. On the other hand, they are prescriptive enough to measure the theological validity of every exegetical approach to Scripture. The interpreter who follows the testimony of the confessional fathers on the principles of Biblical interpretation carries out his task with the confidence that the Holy Spirit will open his eyes to behold "the things of the Spirit of God" (1 Cor. 2:14).

> And after God, through the Holy Spirit in Baptism, has kindled and wrought a beginning of true knowledge of God and faith, we ought to petition him incessantly that by the same Spirit and grace, through daily exercise in reading his Word and putting it into practice, he would preserve faith and his

heavenly gifts in us and strengthen us daily until our end. Unless God himself is our teacher, we cannot study and learn anything pleasing to him and beneficial to us and others. (FC SD II, 16)

CHAPTER 10

Confessional Hermeneutics at the Crossroads

The last 15 years have witnessed, perhaps as never before, the emergence of hermeneutical issues which imperil the very identity of Lutheranism as an authentically evangelical, confessional communion. The form that the Lutheran Church is assuming today, especially in North America, can be determined in no small degree by the answers given to a series of hermeneutical questions. These questions directly concern the nature of the material to be interpreted, and therefore the issues cluster around an understanding of Biblical authority: What is the nature of this authority, and on what is such authority based? What is the relationship between Holy Scripture and the Word of God? What role does the Gospel play in Scripture's authority? Finally, how do the answers to these questions affect the hermeneutical presuppositions and principles with which we practice Biblical exegesis?[1]

The foregoing chapters have duly acknowledged the confessions' reverent view of Holy Scripture as clear, utterly reliable words addressed by God Himself to troubled sinners concerning the redemption He has secured for them in Jesus Christ. Because the Bible is everywhere confessed as the very Word of God, neither Melanchthon, Luther, nor the second-generation drafters of the Formula of Concord would allow for any competing source or norm in their theological enterprise. Rather, both by explicit unequivocal affirmation and by demonstrable practice, the Lutheran Confessions praise and use the Scriptures—with their central witness to Jesus Christ and eternal salvation—as the only source, rule, and norm for any and all statements of doctrine.

Clearly this affirmation of Scripture as the "formal principle" on which our proclamation and theology rest is never an end in itself; rather, the primary function of the inspired Scriptures in the life of the church is to serve as the God-given source and norm for our life-giving use of Word and Sacrament. In this way He frees proclamation, witness, and theology from the liabilities of a purely human determination of what the content of His Gospel and sacraments really is.

A historical-grammatical methodology for the interpretation of Holy Scripture enabled the confessors not only to observe standard rules applicable to any literature (e.g., "Seek the native, literal, or intended sense of the text;" "Derive the meaning from the text," "Let Scripture interpret itself"), but also to retain their distinctive theological emphases regarding Scripture's nature, content, and purpose (namely, that Holy Scripture is God's literary Word about Jesus Christ for our salvation). Since the divine authorship was accomplished through human penmen living and writing as men of their times, the Bible must also be read as a historical volume. At the same time, the confessional exegete who is thus obliged to make use of the principles of historical investigation will always appreciate the divine-human character of every word of Scripture. Historical factors must be enlisted in the service of the Bible's claim about itself as the voice of God speaking Law and Gospel for the gracious justification of all men through faith in Jesus Christ. Since the Holy Spirit is their author and Jesus Christ their principal content, the Scriptures are a literary and theological unit and must be interpreted as such.

Agreement on proper hermeneutical principles cannot be expected without prior accord on the nature of Scripture as God's own Word. This should be self-evident. Yet, while it is conceded that one's hermeneutical method must do justice to the matter to be interpreted,[2] it is precisely this prior agreement on the nature and consequent attributes of Holy Scripture that is lacking in some quarters of Lutheranism today. As a result, there neither is nor can be any genuine consensus on the interpretative procedures to be followed. Without any working controls for our theological hermeneutics—and in the present context the noun should never be considered apart from its qualifying adjective— exegetical anarchy results.

This condition exists at the present time because the discipline is tyrannized by a historical-critical methodology whose theological underpinnings are incompatible with those set forth in this volume. The deep and serious inroads made by historical-critical methodology in contemporary Lutheran hermeneutics stem from two interrelated factors: (1) There is no longer an unqualified recognition of Holy Scripture as the written Word of God, and, consequently, (2) exegetes, with varying degrees of consistency, approach the prophetic and apostolic Scriptures as a primarily *human*—and hence fallible—witness to revelation, subject to the same rules of historical scrutiny as any other human document.

In addressing ourselves directly to these twin factors, we shall in this chapter examine and evaluate some of the more glaring attempts to redefine the relationship between Scripture and the Word of God, reiterate the confessions' relentless insistence on the normative authority of Scripture for the faith and life of the church, explore the inevitable operational presuppositions of historical criticism with a view to assessing their compatibility with a confessional doctrine of Scripture, and, finally, conclude with a set of theses designed to aid those confused and perhaps troubled by the prevalent application of historical-critical methodology to what, when all is said and done, is our singular access to the saving Gospel of Jesus Christ.

Biblical Authority Reexamined

One might debate whether the hermeneutical dilemma that has accompanied the rise of historical criticism is a cause or a result of Lutheranism's perceptible drift from its clear and traditional confession of Holy Scripture as the Word of God. What cannot be disputed, however, is the change in the doctrine of Scripture that is necessarily linked with the adoption of the historical-critical method. The historical critic "presupposes that God's Word is before the Scriptures, is witnessed to in the Scriptures, but is not identical with the Scriptures."[3] In fact, Erich Dinkler's open admission "that the Bible and the Word of

129

God, and that Holy Scripture and the kerygma are not identical is a presupposition of Biblical criticism"[4] is simply a polite application of Johann Salomo Semler's exclamation that "the root of the evil [in theology] is the interchangeable use of the terms 'Scripture' and 'Word of God.'"[5] Those at all familiar with the history of Biblical interpretation will recall the oft-repeated designation of Semler as the "father" of historical-critical theology.[6]

Very often doubts about the nature of Scripture begin with a proper appeal to consider "Word of God" in terms broader than the Bible. The term "Word of God" certainly is also applied to the Gospel, the proclaimed Word, and above all to the Second Person of the Trinity, the incarnate Word. But those proper meanings of "Word of God" do not at all deny the relationship that also exists between Scripture and the Word of God. Nevertheless, precisely this *non sequitur* is advanced by some writers as theological justification for the practice of historical criticism. For example, after sketching the various meanings of "Word of God" in the Bible, Lutheran theologian Warren Quanbeck concluded that, while Scripture is a record and interpretation of revelatory events and thus an instrument of the Holy Spirit possessing the authority of the *Deus loquens,* this is *not* to be understood "as an authority in the Bible itself, based upon claims that the Bible makes for itself."[7] He explains:

> The tendency to regard the Bible as intrinsically authoritative is in danger of centering authority in the book rather than in the God who speaks in the book. This can easily degenerate into a form of idolatry, which is the more perilous because an authoritative book can be manipulated by the theologian. The God who speaks in Scripture cannot, however, be manipulated. He remains sovereign Lord of his creation and of his Church.[8]

The above is typical of the arguments made in support of the Scripture/Word of God disjunction. Other arguments usually include references to the dangers of a growing fundamentalism, the primary Christocentricity of "Word of God," the claims to inspiration made by venerated writings of other religions, and the inability to demonstrate Scriptural authority empirically or through a priori appeals. All of these points are valid, but quite irrelevant to the issue.

Confessional Lutheranism has always stressed that recognition of the divine authority of Holy Scripture is a fruit of our faith in the Gospel of Jesus Christ. Moreover, none of the attributes of Scripture (e.g., inspiration, clarity, uniqueness, efficacy, unity, or infallibility) can ever be conclusively demonstrated either rationally or scientifically. They are articles of faith. At the same time, the *Biblical* content of the Gospel we preach and administer is our assurance that our Gospel message comes from *God*, and therefore expresses *His* will and possesses *His* power. Whatever is faithful to the message of Holy Scripture serves the Gospel, and whatever opposes Holy Scripture threatens the Gospel. As stated elsewhere,

> We submit to the Scriptures as the divinely authoritative Word because our commitment to Christ as Lord has led us to such submission.... Within the sphere of [the] new life [in Christ] our commitment to Scripture arises. This commitment is for us not so much a matter of decision and proof as of submission, for it is part and parcel of the new life which gives up all pride and boasting. The Christ in whom we have found new life is the Christ of the prophetic and apostolic Scriptures, the Christ who bids us to observe whatever he has commanded through his prophets and apostles.[9]

In addition, one needs to be sensitive to the methodology often at work in this discussion. Contemporary Lutheran theologians appeal to Jesus Christ and to the Gospel as the primary meaning of "Word of God," but then use this valid emphasis to detract from the character of Scripture as Word of God without qualification. In this way an altogether false antithesis has been introduced. The authority question is framed as an inappropriate either/or: Is the Bible God's authoritative Word because it announces the Gospel, *or* because it is inspired? This way of asking the question falsely implies that one must choose between mutually exclusive options. Instead, Lutheran theology makes a twofold affirmation: First, as Law and Gospel, the sacred Scriptures are God's powerful instrument for salvation through which

131

the Holy Spirit creates the faith that grasps Christ and frees people from sin and death. Second, as God's inspired Word, these sacred Scriptures regulate our confession, proclamation, and teaching in the church.[10] Having been brought to faith in Jesus Christ, we accept both the testimony about Him that is Holy Scripture and what this testimony says about itself, namely, that it is the very Word of God for our faith and life.[11]

A misguided Scripture/Word of God tension is sometimes emphasized to such an extent that belief in Scripture as the objectively authoritative and truthful written Word of God is actually seen to be an impediment to a living, dynamic relationship with Jesus Christ. What Scripture *does* (especially as Gospel) is stressed to the virtual exclusion of what it *is* (namely, the product of divine inspiration). The authority of Scripture is then said to be derived from its Gospel message rather than from its divine Author. Typical of this view among American Lutherans is Paul G. Bretscher, who writes: "The Word of God, meaning Christ and the Gospel which proclaims Him, is the true glory and authority of the Bible. For the sake of that message it is proper to call the Holy Scriptures 'the Word of God.'"[12] He explains:

> When the cross has been left behind, Lutheran education will hold to "the Word of God" in a single meaning of that phrase. The Word of God is the message, formulated in human words, which God addresses to our hearts out of the cross of Christ. Its closest synonym would be the term "Gospel," whether in the narrow focus of absolution (the pronouncement of forgiveness), or in a wider sense that takes in all articles of Christian confession, or in the widest sense that includes also God's Word of Law and wrath. Scripture is properly called "the Word of God," then, for the sake of the Gospel of truth and life in Christ which is its glory. Because of this message the Scriptures are our pure and clear fountain and our only rule and norm for faith and life.[13]

Apparently such descriptions are intended to prevent one from emphasizing the form of Holy Scripture *(verba)* at the expense of its redemptive, Christological substance *(res)*. But has any Lutheran Church body or theologian really made this mistake? How often must one deny that he has made "the doctrine of the inspiration or the inerrancy of the Scriptures a prior truth which guarantees the truth of the Gospel"? Furthermore, no responsible Lutheran theologian has ever maintained that we are saved through a combination of faith in Christ and faith in the Bible.[14] Had God not first revealed Himself in His Son, the Bible would remain a dark and utterly ineffective book, much as the Old Testament was veiled to the disciples until Christ opened it to them by demonstrating how the Law and the Prophets had been fulfilled in Him (Luke 24:44-46).[15] The simple and magnificent fact is this: The Gospel which is the center of our theology is the Gospel to which the Scriptures bear witness, while the Scriptures from which we derive our theology direct us steadfastly to the Gospel of Jesus Christ.[16] Formal and material principles are therefore both rooted in Christ; they should be distinguished but never separated.[17]

Those who fail to maintain this Biblical and undeniably confessional[18] connection (that is, that Scripture is in fact the written Word of God) and who have redefined Scriptural authority along purely functional lines have thereby also disclosed something extremely important about their hermeneutical presuppositions.[19] By deliberately limiting the identification between Scripture and Word of God in order to permit the use of historical-critical methodology, they have tacitly admitted that this method cannot properly be applied to the Word of God.[20] If Scripture is called Word of God only in terms of its function and not therefore also in terms of its nature, one is free to study the Bible with the same methods used on all ancient literature, namely, with the historical-critical method.[21] The issue is well stated by Samuel Nafzger:

> What is this book that is to be interpreted? Is it the very Word of God in the words of men, or is it *only* the fallible witness of human beings to God's revelation of Himself in history through which He somehow continues to speak? Is Scripture itself revelation, or is it *only* the occasion for revelation to take place once again? Is the root of the evil in theology the interchangeable use of the terms *Scripture* and *Word of God* (Semler), or is the root of the problem the wedge that has been drawn between them.[22]

This perception of the issue is supported by the recent literary exchange between Peter Stuhlmacher of Tuebingen and his former student, Gerhard Maier. In *The End of the Historical-Critical Method* Maier assumed an incarnational approach to the problem of historical criticism and insisted that "the Bible itself gives no key with which to distinguish between the Word of God and Scripture, and along with that, between Christ and Scripture."[23] This meant that the historical-critical method, as a matter of basic principle, requires that the Bible must be approached from an extra-Biblical position and with extra-Biblical standards; the objective is to discover the Word of God in the process.[24] Maier's distaste for the idea of finding an inner Word of God within the Biblical canon led to his conclusion that the historical-critical method was bound to fail because it was not suited to the subject.[25] He explains:

> Use of the historical-critical method divided the Bible forcibly into two Bibles, one human and one divine. In spite of honest endeavor, as a result of the lack of a "key," agreement was never reached as to what firmly and always would have to be considered a part of "divine truths."[26]

In short, the very concept and development of historical-critical methodology "present an inner impossibility to the extent that one holds to the position that the witness of divine revelation is presented in the canonical Scriptures."[27]

Peter Stuhlmacher appreciated the gravity of this criticism and responded to Maier's contention in *Historical Criticism and Theological Interpretation of Scripture.* He suggested that Maier "would rather retreat behind the historical-scientific ranking of the biblical books with other ancient sources (made since Semler) and behind the distinction between the scriptural text and the word of God (in use since Semler) to an evaluation of the biblical canon as the inerrant source of revelation and the inspired word of God."[28] In contrast to this alleged "retreat," Stuhlmacher argued that in view of the "ever increasing abundance of insight concerning the origin and uniqueness of Holy Scripture," the resolution to employ the historical-critical method is "irrevocable."[29] While Stuhlmacher urges a "hermeneutics of consent" (roughly equivalent to historical criticism's much acclaimed but nebulously defined "capacity for self-correction")[30] to augment the classical Troeltschian axioms,[31] it is clear that his refusal to identify Scripture with the Word of God permits him to advocate the continued use of the historical-critical method. On the other hand, Maier's unequivocal identification of Scripture with the Word of God prompts him to reject the method in principle.[32]

Exegetes of varying persuasions concede that the nature of the writing to be explained to a great extent affects one's interpretive framework, and that the Word of God as such is not open to criticism. Therefore, advocates of a historical-critical approach to the Scriptures have had to come to a prior conclusion about the character of Holy Scripture, namely, that the Scriptures are not themselves Word of God but only "contain," "witness to," or "become" Word of God. The Bible is not the written Word of God without qualification. Hence it can be approached by means of historical-critical methodology. Kurt Marquart correctly observes:

> Since it is self-contradictory to take issue with God's Word, but since the right to take issue with biblical statements is an inherent, constitutive necessity for the historical-critical method . . . it is clear that the application of criticism to Scripture cannot be justified so long as the biblical writings are regarded as inviolable, divinely inspired truth given in human language. That is why, as we have seen, Semler declared, "The root of evil is the confusion of Scripture and Word of God." Before any historical-critical operation can begin, a wedge must first be driven between that which is divine and that which is human in Scripture.[33]

Such limitations of Scriptural authority as we have noted are entirely foreign to the Lutheran Confessions. There is absolutely no question that the confessions do identify Scripture with Word of God. In the closest thing to a section on the doctrine of Scripture in the *Book of Concord,* the Formula's Summary Rule and Norm, the prophetic and apostolic writings of the Old and New Testaments are expressly called "the pure and clear fountain of Israel, which is the only true norm according to which all teachers and teachings are to be judged and evaluated" (SD Rule and Norm, 3). The term "fountain" *(Brunnen)* depicts Scripture as the source of all theology, while the twin adjectives "clear" and "pure" acknowledge the Bible's perspicuity and truthfulness. But the Formula calls Scripture more than just the source of all doctrine; it is *judge* and *norm* as well. The term "judge" *(Richter, iudex),* Robert Preus correctly notes, "is a deliberate hypostatization, indicating that Scripture carries out *God's* own function in the church on earth, the function of judging teachers and teaching." [34]

The normative authority of Scripture is self-evidently a divine authority. The fountain of Israel—the source of the will, mysteries, and thoughts of God—is a divine source. Only God—or His Word—can judge all doctrine in the church.

> In this way the distinction between the Holy Scripture of the Old and New Testaments and all other writings is maintained, and Holy Scripture remains the only judge, rule, and norm according to which as the only touchstone all doctrines should and must be understood and judged as good or evil, right or wrong.
>
> Other symbols and other writings are not judges like Holy Scripture, but merely witnesses and expositions of the faith, setting forth how at various times the Holy Scriptures were understood by contemporaries in the church of God with reference to controverted articles, and how contrary teachings were rejected and condemned. (FC Rule and Norm, 7-8)

Just as God is the only source of all theology, so His Word, Holy Scripture, is for us the only source of our knowledge of theology. Similarly, just as God must be judge over everything taught in His name, so His Scriptural Word is the exclusive judge and norm available to the church whereby teachers and doctrines can be judged.[35]

The Formula does not detach the section concerning the function of Scripture as the Word of God from the 12 doctrinal articles which follow. Instead, the affirmation of Scripture as the Word of God, and thus as source and judge of all ecclesiastical teaching, establishes a principle of interpretation which the writers intend to observe faithfully throughout their exposition of

136

controverted doctrines. The normative authority of Scripture is acknowledged and followed throughout the Formula,[36] just as it is in the earlier confessional writings.

It is a basic hermeneutical precept when treating any writing which claims to speak authoritatively on a particular issue to determine who its author is and the degree of authority it is to be given. There is no possible doubt in any of the confessional literature about the relationship between the divine origin of Scripture and its normative authority. Holy Scripture is the exclusive authority for doctrine in the church because it is the Word of God Himself.[37]

Historical-Critical Methodology and Lutheran Confessional Hermeneutics

What is it about the historical-critical method that makes it so inappropriate for sound confessional exegesis? Any attempt to understand or evaluate the theological propriety of the historical-critical method must first overcome the confusion that all too often surrounds the term. Historical criticism does *not* mean simply reading the ancient Biblical documents in the context of their original historical setting.[38] Any responsible exegesis follows this procedure. Rather, historical criticism, a child of Enlightenment rationalism, treats historical sources (in this case the inspired Scriptural writings) like witnesses in a court of law. The witnesses must be interrogated and their answers evaluated. This interrogation and assessment is called "criticism."[39]

Furthermore, because the historical-critical method is "anything but a carefully defined and agreed on set of axioms and presuppositions,"[40] the consistent application of which yields universally accepted results, the definition must be examined further. The student even remotely familiar with the products of critical Biblical scholarship is well aware of the diverse positions taken on such significant issues as the presence of predictive Messianic prophecy in the Old Testament, the historicity of certain miracle accounts, or the authenticity of Jesus' words in the gospels. Some scholars reach negative answers to these

137

questions; others treat them with comparative restraint and fidelity to the Scriptural text. What accounts for this disparity?

Such varied results must be attributed to the degree of consistency with which the exegete uses the basic principles of criticism. For instance, a form or redaction critic will evaluate a particular saying of Jesus according to how closely he follows or deviates from the most stringent criterion of that branch of New Testament criticism, namely, that authentic sayings of Jesus are said to be limited to those which cannot plausibly be placed into the mouth of contemporary Judaism and which cannot be ascribed to the historical circumstances of the post-Easter church. Involved here are what have been labeled the "wider critical principle" and the "narrow critical principle." The wider principle is basically synonymous with the approach developed by Ernst Troeltsch.[41] The narrow principle constitutes "the bare irreducible minimum of the historical-critical method, which cannot be surrendered without destroying the method itself." [42] If one operates with the wider principle and its essential premises of systematic criticism, analogy, and universal correlation, he will assume, as Soulen correctly notes,

> that reality is uniform and universal, that it is accessible to human reason and investigation, that all events historical and natural occurring within it are in principle comparable by analogy, and that man's contemporary experience of reality can provide the objective criteria by which what could or could not have happened in the past is to be determined.[43]

Those working with the narrow critical principle reject these positivistic excesses and argue that no naturalistic biases are involved. Nevertheless, the self-designated "neutral" critic practices the same art of interrogation and evaluation. He treats the Biblical documents like witnesses to be interrogated or cross-examined, and whose answers must be evaluated. One needs to consider the attitude that underlies a procedure treating Holy Scripture as a defendant before a judge. The exegete might arrive at ostensibly "conservative" conclusions on a wide spectrum of isagogical and interpretative issues, and still the *sola Scriptura* axiom has been quietly but irretrievably abandoned because the *historian* has conferred authority upon the Biblical witness. He has reserved the right "to judge who or what will be called an authority, and he makes this judgment only after he has subjected the so-called witness to a rigorous cross-examination."[44] This prerogative is what Van Harvey calls the "autonomy of the historian," the presupposition underlying *all* historical-critical investigation:

> The historian, in short, is radically autonomous because of the nature of historical knowledge itself. If the historian permits his authorities to stand uncriticized, he abdicates his role as critical historian. He is no longer a seeker of knowledge but a mediator of past belief; not a thinker but a transmitter of tradition.[45]

Whenever the critic confers authority on the witness, he has granted the possibility that the witness might not be reliable. The historian's reason decides whether or not an account is to be taken at face value. When this happens, the authority the Bible possesses as God's written Word has been subverted, and the Holy Scriptures have come to be treated exactly like all other ancient literature. Such treatment is, in the final analysis, the narrow critical principle or least common denominator of historical-critical methodology.

Clearly, one will need to reject what is essential to the confessional Lutheran hermeneutic (specifically, the confessors' view of the nature, content, and purpose of Scripture) if he is to accept and use in any consistent way the historical-critical method and apply it to the Biblical text. By approaching the Scriptures in precisely the same way one approaches other ancient literature, the historical-critical method has set itself apart from the express confessional view which regards Holy Scripture as being uniquely from God. Since this basic approach is antithetical to the hermeneutical presuppositions of the Lutheran Symbols, the two exegetical methods are utterly irreconcilable. Historical criticism cannot be rehabilitated for use in a confessional Lutheran context. Marquart is correct:

> Either *sola sacra scriptura* will be *iudex* or else critical human reason and scholarship, but not both. The two principles are

139

mutually exclusive. One must inevitably rule and the other serve; one function magisterially, the other ministerially. The issue is nonnegotiable. *Tertium non datur.*[46]

Admittedly, several objections have been voiced regarding the description and evaluation of historical criticism developed in these pages. We have argued that at its core historical criticism represents a cross-examination of the Biblical text according to which the individual exegete—not the prophetic and apostolic Scriptures themselves—is invested with ultimate authority. Therefore, this method cannot be employed legitimately by an interpreter who claims, with the confessions, that the Scriptures are the written Word of God. In response, Lutheran proponents of historical criticism maintain that the method itself is neutral, and that they practice historical criticism "with Lutheran presuppositions." This disclaimer, however, fails to realize that one's choice of exegetical tools reveals a predisposition about the nature of the material to be interpreted. The stubborn fact is that the hermeneutical presuppositions of historical criticism and of the historical-grammatical method of the Lutheran Confessions are incompatible. Any claim to use the former method with Lutheran presuppositions is either linguistic subterfuge or an implicit rejection of the single criterion which defines criticism. One hopes that the latter is the case, and that the term "historical criticism" is either used carelessly or without realizing what the method as such actually involves.

To be sure, there are those who claim to use "historical criticism" and who are at the same time sincerely committed to a confessional doctrine of Scripture. This highlights the problem which arises from the use of different definitions. Confusion, uncertainty, and distrust are bound to result. Clarification, honesty, and openness on both sides of the critical divide are mandatory. At the same time, those who claim to retain both the Lutheran view of Scripture and historical criticism must face the hard reality that this tenuous balance is seldom, if ever, attempted outside of Lutheran circles. Moreover, integrity demands a complete willingness to spell out precisely how one approaches Biblical exegesis. Very likely this will demonstrate that either the confessional doctrine of Holy Scripture or the essence of historical-critical methodology has been subtly compromised.

Yet another disclaimer is voiced by those who suggest that criticism is required because of the thoroughly historical character of God's revelation. Failure to use the method is said to betray the Gospel by suggesting that the Bible cannot stand the test of historical investigation.[47] Stated in its baldest form, such refusal is held to be a manifestation of the docetic heresy.[48] Again, the real issue here is not whether to use historical investigation in Biblical exegesis, but rather what kind of historical study is to be undertaken. Shall historical data be used ministerially to *explain* the authoritative Scriptural text, or shall historical criticism magisterially *determine* the relative authority of a particular text?

Since God has graciously deigned to reveal Himself through such concrete historical events as exodus, exile, and, above all, incarnation and resurrection, the Biblical witness to these deeds in the plan of salvation demands conscientious and painstaking historical study. But the assertion that rejection of historical criticism is a form of the docetic aberration rests on the dubious circular argument that only what is arrived at through historical-critical investigation can be called historical. This, however, is precisely the point at issue, and one which the confessional exegete—who insists that Scripture is the very Word of God and not merely a predominantly human chronicle of divine activity—can under no circumstances allow. Inasmuch as the use of historical methods is never entirely objective or free of presuppositions, it is important that our presuppositions be Biblical and that our understanding of history itself be derived from and shaped by God's revelation.

Equally wanting is the rationale that "the techniques associated with 'historical-critical' methodology... are legitimated by the fact that God chose to use as His written Word human documents written by human beings in human language."[49] No one disputes the profoundly human dimension everywhere present in both the Old and New Testaments. However, while God accommodated Himself to human speech in giving us the Scriptures (and we thank God that He did)—just as He truly became a

141

man in Jesus Christ—He did not accommodate Himself to human falsehood any more than our Lord accommodated Himself to sin. One might plausibly argue that in some rare instances the procedures common to historical criticism can be purged of their philosophical underpinnings and used with profit in a confessional Lutheran context (e.g., identifying certain New Testament pericopes as early liturgical or creedal formulations), but this does not signal a retreat from the confessional antipathy for any approach to the Scriptures which regards them as human compositions over which the interpreter sits in judgment.[50] Accordingly, the oft-repeated call to read Holy Scripture on its own terms is to be endorsed only when it is recognized that such terms include its divine authorship and consequent truthfulness.

Perhaps the weakest argument of historical critics is the contention that negative judgments about this or that portion of Scripture are not to be feared because these appraisals concern matters peripheral or incidental to the central doctrinal affirmations in the Bible, usually understood as the Law/Gospel dynamic or the Gospel message in its most narrow sense. But the Law/Gospel distinction and the doctrine of justification are not norms in the practice of Biblical interpretation; they are *the message* of Scripture, not free-floating principles to be applied to a passage in order to derive meaning from it. Nor are these cardinal dogmas ever used by the confessions in a reductionistic way, as though any interpretation is legitimate as long as it does not contradict the doctrine of justification or confuse Law and Gospel. In one important sense, the Gospel is norm in the Scriptures, yet Holy Scripture is the source and norm of theology for the sake of the Gospel. The Missouri Synod's Commission on Theology and Church Relations explains in greater detail:

> When Lutherans say that the Gospel is the norm in the Scriptures, they do not mean that so long as the Gospel is not negated it is permissible to employ a method of Bible study which calls into question Lutheran presuppositions about the kind of a book the Bible is, or which in any way qualifies the authority of *all* Scripture. . . .
>
> The Gospel is the norm in the Scriptures in the sense that it absolutely prohibits understanding any passage to teach sal-

vation by works. It is *not* norm in the sense that the center of Scripture becomes a device to sanction a view of the Bible and a method of interpreting it which virtually denies that the *whole* Bible is God's inspired, authoritative Word on all matters concerning which it speaks.[51]

Aside from the sobering realization that the supposed discovery of marginal "errors" has led inevitably to misgivings about substantive theological matters, there is a still more central objection to this whole enterprise: Any retreat from historical or "factual" matters may well be a retreat from the incarnation.[52] Indeed, the historical dimension of revelation and its saving purpose are inextricably intertwined. Any position which separates them must necessarily bring in some external criterion for determining which portions of Scripture are "doctrinal" and which are not.[53] One thing is absolutely certain: The attempt to wrench theological or spiritual truth from its grounding in history finds no support or precedent in Scripture itself. Instead, the separation between faith and fact, between theology and history, while deeply anti-incarnational, is basic to the historical-critical method.[54]

A final comment must address the important issue of how confessional *subscription* relates to the exegesis of the Lutheran Confessions. To state that "we are not bound to the exegesis of the confessions" is, as it stands, a half-truth open to a good deal of misunderstanding. We are not bound to every selection of passages the symbols make in support of a particular doctrine, nor to every detail in their interpretation of specific passages. Yet having acknowledged this, it must at once be added that we cannot reject the exegetical conclusions of the confessions without thereby abandoning the *Book of Concord* itself as a normative doctrinal entity based upon the explicit, clear testimony of Holy Scripture. Progressive, systematic rejection of the passages supporting articles of faith, or an overhaul of the exegetical methodology of the confessions by means of historical criticism, is little short of a repudiation of the symbols themselves.[55] Horace Hummel explains: "We must distinguish carefully between . . . the mere details of the interpretation and application of isolated passages or the precise way in which their thrust is restated, and

143

... such material changes as would simply constitute a different 'confession' of what we understand the Scriptures to be saying."[56]

Conclusion

We might, then, identify the following principles for Biblical interpretation in a Lutheran confessional context:

1. Subscription to the Lutheran Confessions includes acceptance of the confessional position on the nature and interpretation of Holy Scripture.

2. Holy Scripture is the product of the unique and miraculous action of God the Holy Spirit upon His chosen prophets and apostles whereby He spoke His Word in their words, so that He is the true author of their every word. Because of their divine authorship, the Scriptures are qualitatively different from every other form of human expression in every age. Therefore, while "Word of God" is a more comprehensive term than Holy Scripture, Scripture is nevertheless Word of God.

3. God addresses men and women in Law and Gospel throughout Scripture in order to lead them to salvation through faith in Jesus Christ. The *sola scriptura* principle focuses on the unfolding of Scripture's Christological content for its soteriological purpose.

4. The Christian accepts the claim of the Scriptures to be the Word of God because he has first been brought to faith in Jesus Christ by the power of the Holy Spirit working through the means of grace.

5. Because the Scriptures were authored by God they address man as God's own infallible, powerful, and authoritative speech. As such the Scriptures are the only source and norm for all doctrine in the church, serving the "purely" and "rightly" of the church's use of Word and Sacrament (cf. AC VII).

6. Inasmuch as the same God speaks the same message of Christ and his salvation throughout the Scriptures, the Scriptures present an organic unity of doctrine both within and between the Old and New Testaments. The unity of authorship, content, and purpose, is reflected in the principle that Scripture interprets Scripture, whether applied to individual passages or articles of faith.

144

7. Since God's authorship of Holy Scripture was accomplished through human authors living and writing at various times and places as men of their times, the Scriptures must be read as historical, literary documents in order to discern God's intended meaning. This meaning is to be sought in the text, not behind it or apart from it. Careful literary exegesis is therefore not an option but a necessity for the Christian interpreter. Moreover, while the Bible is fundamentally clear in its language, we must have the Holy Spirit in order to understand its message.

8. Because the historical-critical method by definition treats the sacred Scriptures no differently than any other ancient literature, involving a cross-examination of the text which makes the individual exegete and not the Biblical witness the ultimate authority, the method as such is absolutely incompatible with both the *sola scriptura* principle and with an unconditional, *quia* subscription to the Lutheran Confessions.

9. The Law-Gospel distinction and the doctrine of justification not only serve to clarify passages dealing with faith and works but are basic presuppositions for the interpretation of all Scripture, without, however, providing general criteria for the correctness or legitimacy of particular exegetical interpretations.

The Lutheran Confessions clearly accept and teach the causative and normative authority of Holy Scripture and the hermeneutical principles which that view requires. For the confessions—and for us—all Biblical interpretation must serve the high and noble purpose of heralding to the world the Good News of God in Jesus Christ.

Viewed in that Gospel light, the recognition and use of Holy Scripture as the very Word of God is not simply an end in itself, but a vital, not to be relinquished, dimension of the church's faithfulness to its primary mission.

Notes

INTRODUCTION

1. "Articles of Incorporation" and "Constitution of the Lutheran Church—Missouri Synod," Article II, in *Handbook of the Lutheran Church—Missouri Synod* (St. Louis: Concordia Publishing House, 1966), pp. 11, 15.
2. For example, some Lutherans in the Danish-Norwegian tradition. For a detailed discussion of the confessional commitments of the various churches in world Lutheranism, see Hans Weissgerber, "The Valid Confessional Symbols," in *The Church and the Confessions: The Role of the Confessions in the Life and Doctrine of the Lutheran Churches*, ed. Vilmos Vajta and Hans Weissgerber (Philadelphia: Fortress Press, 1963), pp. 1—22.
3. "Constitution," Art. II.
4. From "The Order for the Ordination of a Minister," in *The Lutheran Liturgy* (St. Louis: Concordia Publishing House, n.d.), pp. 106—07.
5. "Constitution of The American Lutheran Church, Article IV. Confession of Faith," in *Documents of Lutheran Unity in America*, ed. Richard C. Wolf (Philadelphia: Fortress Press, 1966), p. 533.
6. "Article II. Confession of Faith," *Constitution and By-Laws, Lutheran Church in America, Including Amendments to By-Laws Adopted at the 1964 Convention of the Church* (Philadelphia: Board of Publication, Lutheran Church in America, n.d.), p. 3. While the concept of the Confessions as Biblical expositions is not explicit in this article, it nevertheless appears that the Confessions are viewed as witnesses to the Gospel transmitted in the Scripture, and not as norms independent of Holy Scripture.
7. "Constitution of the Lutheran World Federation, Article II. Doctrinal Basis," in *Lutheran World Federation, Proceedings of the Fourth Assembly of the Lutheran World Federation, Helsinki, July 30 to August 11, 1963* (Berlin und Hamburg: Lutherisches Verlagshaus, 1965), pp. 296 and 402.
8. "Constitution of the Lutheran Council in the United States of America, Preamble," in *Convention Workbook (Reports and Overtures), 46th Regular Convention, The Lutheran Church—Missouri Synod, Detroit, Michigan, June 16—26, 1965* [St. Louis: Concordia Publishing House, 1965], p. 44.
9. "Die andere *Symbola* aber und angezogene Schriften sind nicht Richter wie die Heilige Schrift, sondern allein Zeugnis und Erklaerung des Glaubens, wie jederzeit die Heilige Schrift in streitigen Artikuln in der Kirchen Gottes von den damals Lebenden verstanden und ausgeleget, und derselben widerwaertige Lehr vorworfen und vordambt worden." The German text is from *Die Bekenntnisschriften der evangelisch-lutherischen Kirche* (5th rev. ed.; Goettingen: Vandenhoeck & Ruprecht, 1963), p. 769, 28—35.
10. "Preface," *The Book of Concord*, ed. Theodore G. Tappert (Philadelphia: Fortress Press, 1959), pp. 8, 6, 7, 12, and 13.
11. Helmut Echternach, "Schriftprinzip und Bekenntnis," *Evangelisch-klutherische Kirchenzeitung*, V (Feb. 15, 1951), 38.
12. "wird allein dahin gemeint, dass man habe eine einhellige, gewisse,

allgemeine Form der Lehre, darzu sich unsere evangelische Kirchen saembtlich und ingemein bekennen, aus und nach welcher, weil sie aus Gottes Word genommen, alle andere Schriften, wiefern sie zu probieren und anzunehmen, geurteilt und reguliert sollen werden." *Bekenntnisschriften*, p. 838, 6—14.

13. See FC Ep Rule and Norm, 1 and 7; FC SD Rule and Norm, 3.

14. Edmund Schlink, *Theology of the Lutheran Confessions*, trans. P. F. Koehneke and H. J. A. Bouman (Philadelphia: Muhlenberg Press, 1961), p. xvi.

15. Ibid., p. 12.

16. Ibid., p. xix.

17. See Wilhelm C. Linss, "Biblical Interpretation in the Formula of Concord," in *The Symposium on Seventeenth Century Lutheranism, I* (St. Louis: The Symposium on Seventeenth Century Lutheranism, 1962), 118—35; Juergen Roloff, "The Interpretation of Scripture in Article IV of Melanchthon's Apology of the Augsburg Confession," *Lutheran World*, VIII (1961), 47—63; and Schlink, pp. 297—317.

18. Schlink states: "Furthermore, in the actual use of Scripture by the Confessions there is implicit not only a doctrine of Scripture, but also principles of interpretation, and even important hermeneutical rules for the exegesis of the Old Testament" (p. 1, n. 1).

19. Arthur Carl Piepkorn, "Suggested Principles for a Hermeneutics of the Lutheran Symbols," *Concordia Theological Monthly*, XXIX (January 1958), 6.

20. Above, n. 10.

Chapter 1

1. Wilhelm F. Schmidt and K. Schornbaum, *Die Fraenkischen Bekenntnisse. Eine Vorstufe der Augsburgischen Konfession*, publ. by Landeskirchenrat der evang.-luth. Kirche in Bayern (Munich: Chr. Kaiser Verlag, 1930), p. 184.

2. Ibid., p. 186.

3. Ibid.

4. Ibid., p. 66.

5. Ibid., pp. 413—27.

6. Ibid., pp. 463—64.

7. Werner Elert, *The Structure of Lutheranism*, trans. Walter A. Hansen (St. Louis: Concordia Publishing House, 1962), p. 183.

8. Edmund Schlink, *Theology of the Lutheran Confessions*, trans. P. F. Koehneke and H. J. A. Bouman (Philadelphia: Muhlenberg Press, 1961), pp. 5—6.

9. Ibid., p. 2, n.

10. Ibid., p. 6.

11. Elert, pp. 190—91.

12. F. E. Mayer, *The Religious Bodies of America*, 4th ed., rev. Arthur Carl Piepkorn (St. Louis: Concordia Publishing House, 1961), p. 144.

13. Ibid., p. 145.

14. Ibid., pp. 145—46.

15. Arthur Carl Piepkorn, "The Position of the Church and Her Symbols," in "Essays on the Inspiration of Scripture," *Concordia Theological Monthly*, XXV (October 1954), 740.

16. Holsten Fagerberg, *A New Look at the Lutheran Confessions (1529—1537)*, trans. Gene J. Lund (St. Louis: Concordia Publishing House, 1972), p. 15.

17. M. Reu, *Luther and the Scriptures* (Columbus, Ohio: The Wartburg Press,

1944), reprinted in *The Springfielder,* XXIV (August 1960), 70. A similar position is set forth by Wilhelm Walther, *Das Erbe der Reformation im Kampf der Gegenwart,* I (Leipzig: A. Deichert'sche Verlagsbuchhandlung, 1903), 56—94. The accent on divine authorship is deemphasized by Karl Holl, "Luthers Bedeutung fuer den Fortschritt der Auslegungskunst," *Gesammelte Aufsaetze zur Kirchengeschichte,* I, *Luther,* (6th ed.; Tuebingen: J. C. B. Mohr, 1927), 544 to 582. For a recent survey of Luther research on this point, see John Warwick Montgomery, "Lutheran Hermeneutics and Hermeneutics Today," in *Aspects of Biblical Hermeneutics: Confessional Principles and Practical Applications,* Occasional Papers No. 1 of *Concordia Theological Monthly* (St. Louis: Concordia Publishing House, 1966), pp. 91—102.

18. Ibid., p. 11.

19. See *Canons and Decrees of the Council of Trent,* trans. H. J. Schroeder (St. Louis: B. Herder Book Co., 1950), pp. 17—18, for the Roman Catholic list of canonical books. Among the many Reformed confessions, the following contain a list of canonical Scriptures: *Zuericher Bekenntnis* (1545), *Confessio gallicana* (1559), *Confessio belgica* (1561), the *Thirty-nine Articles* (1562), and the *Westminster Confession* (1647). See *Die Bekenntnisschriften der reformierten Kirche,* ed. E. F. Karl Mueller (Leipzig: A. Deichert'sche Verlagsbuchhandlung, 1903), pp. 155, 222, 233, 507, and 543 respectively.

20. Schlink, p. 9.

21. Cf. "Verzeichnis der zitierten Schriftstellen" in *Die Bekenntnisschriften der evangelisch-lutherischen Kirche,* 5th rev. ed. (Goettingen: Vandenhoeck & Ruprecht, 1963), pp. 1137—44.

22. According to the table of Biblical references in *The Book of Concord,* ed. T. G. Tappert (Philadelphia: Fortress Press, 1959), pp. 639—48.

23. Ibid., p. 19. The Latin text reads: "Et in spiritum sanctum . . . qui locutus est per prophetas," *Bekenntnisschriften,* p. 27.

24. "Amplectimur etiam tria illa catholica et generalia summae auctoritatis symbola. . . ." (FC SD Rule and Norm, 4).

25. J. N. D. Kelly, *Early Christian Creeds,* 2d ed. (London: Longmans, Green, and Co., Ltd., 1960), pp. 183—84.

26. Ibid., p. 341.

27. The translation in *The Book of Concord* omits the word "gottlicher." Cf. AC Preface, 8, p. 25.

28. Cf., e.g., *The Book of Concord,* p. 3, lines 13 and 25; p. 5, lines 6 and 19; p. 11, line 19; and p. 12, lines 5, 24, and 42.

29. Cf. ibid. p. 4, line 27; p. 6, lines 26 and 35; and p. 13, line 23.

30. The language of this citation is strikingly similar to a formula employed in the New Testament to introduce quotations from the Old Testament. For example, see Acts 3:18, "which God before had showed by the mouth of all His prophets"; Acts 3:21, "which God hath spoken by the mouth of all His holy prophets since the world began"; Acts 4:24-25, "God . . . who by the mouth of Thy servant David hast said"; and Luke 1:70, "as He spake by the mouth of His holy prophets, which have been since the world began."

31. Fagerberg, p. 17.

32. Ibid., p. 19.

33. Ibid., p. 22.

34. Luther equated Scripture and *ius divinum:* "Sacra scriptura, quae est proprie jus divinum [Holy Scripture, which is properly divine command]." Cited in *Die Bekenntnisschriften der evangelisch-lutherischen Kirche,* p. 427, n. 3.

35. Cf. FC SD X, 15: "welchen zu erhalten der Heilige Geist durch den Mund des heiligen Apostels seiner Kirchen, wie jtzt gehoert, so ernstlich befohlen hat."

36. Piepkorn, "Position," *Concordia Theological Monthly,* pp. 740—41.

Chapter 2

1. This reference to Romans 15:4 includes the New Testament within the scope of "Scripture," as the confessional context makes clear.
2. The original German reads: "und bleibt allein die Heilige Schrift der einig Richter, Regel und Richtschnur, nach welcher als dem einigen Probierstein sollen und muessen alle Lehren erkannt und geurteilt werden, ob sie gut oder boes, recht oder unrecht sein." In *Die Bekenntnisschriften der evangelisch-lutherischen Kirche*, 5th rev. ed. (Goettingen: Vandenhoeck & Ruprecht, 1963), p. 769.
3. Peter Fraenkel, *Testimonia Patrum: The Function of the Patristic Argument in the Theology of Philip Melanchthon* (Geneva: Libraire E. Droz, 1961), p. 190, n. 83. Fraenkel supports this statement with references to Melanchthon's "Preface to the Greek Bible," Cranmer's dedicatory epistle to Flacius' *De Voce et Re Fidei*, dedication verses in a German Bible for Martin Luther, Jr., and two statements from Luther's writings.
4. Holsten Fagerberg, *A New Look at the Lutheran Confessions (1529—1537)*, trans. Gene J. Lund (St. Louis: Concordia Publishing House, 1972), p. 16.
5. Ibid., p. 15.
6. According to the table of Biblical references in *The Book of Concord*, ed. T. G. Tappert (Philadelphia: Fortress Press, 1959), pp. 639—48.
7. Fagerberg, p. 16.
8. "Preface," *The Book of Concord*, pp. 4, 5, 8, and 12.
9. Note the Latin translation: "porro autem verbum Dei nec potest errare nec fallere," *Bekenntnisschriften*, p. 703.
10. "Preface," *The Book of Concord*, pp. 5—6, 13, 11, and 12.
11. Edmund Schlink, *Theology of the Lutheran Confessions*, trans. P. F. Koehneke and H. J. A. Bouman (Philadelphia: Muhlenberg Press, 1961), pp. 6 and 8. Cf. also p. 220, "The norm of the church is the proclaimed Biblical Gospel."
12. Fagerberg, pp. 30—31.
13. Ibid., p. 33.

Chapter 3

1. Martin Luther, *The Bondage of the Will*, trans. J. I. Packer and O. R. Johnston (Westwood, N. J.: Fleming H. Revell Company, 1957), p. 71. For a detailed examination of this concept in *Bondage of the Will*, see Rudolf Hermann, *Von der Klarheit der heiligen Schrift: Untersuchungen und Eroerterungen ueber Luthers Lehre von der Schrift in De servo arbitrio* (Berlin: Evangelische Verlagsanstalt, 1958).
2. Ibid., p. 128.
3. Ibid.
4. Ibid., pp. 73—74; cf. also p. 124.
5. Ibid., p. 71.
6. Ibid., p. 77.
7. Gerhard Krause, *Studien zu Luthers Auslegung der Kleinen Propheten* (Tuebingen: J. C. B. Mohr, 1962), p. 268.
8. Ibid., p. 281.
9. Peter Fraenkel, *Testimonia Patrum: The Function of the Patristic Argument in the Theology of Philip Melanchthon* (Geneva: Libraire E. Droz, 1961), pp. 209—10.
10. Martin Chemnitz, "Concerning the Interpretation of the Scripture," *Examination of the Council of Trent*, Part I, trans. Fred Kramer, (St. Louis: Concordia Publishing House, 1971), pp. 207—08.
11. See, e.g., FC SD II, 10—14; FC SD XI, 27—32; and SA, II, i.

12. The German translation is more explicit: "wider die oeffentliche helle Schrift und klare Word des heil. Geistes." In *Die Bekenntnisschriften der evangelisch-lutherischen Kirche* (5th rev. ed.; Goettingen: Vandenhoeck & Ruprecht, 1963), p. 143.
13. Norman Habel, *The Form and Meaning of the Fall Narrative: A Detailed Analysis of Genesis 3* (St. Louis: Concordia Seminary Print Shop, 1965), p. 1.

Chapter 4

1. Holsten Fagerberg demonstrates satisfactorily that the word Gospel as it is used in the confessions often denotes the New Testament as such or content of the New Testament; thus the word Gospel not only is closely related to the Scriptures, but also on occasion denotes a portion of Scripture. In *A New Look at the Lutheran Confessions (1529—1537)*, trans. Gene J. Lund (St. Louis: Concordia Publishing House, 1972), pp. 88—93.
2. Edmund Schlink, *Theology of the Lutheran Confessions*, trans. P. F. Koehneke and H. J. A. Bouman (Philadelphia: Muhlenberg Press, 1961), pp. 136—37.
3. Cf. Articles II—IX, XI, XII, XV, XVII, XVIII, XX, XXI, and XXIV.
4. Herbert J. A. Bouman, "Some Thoughts on the Theological Presuppositions for a Lutheran Approach to the Scriptures," in *Aspects of Biblical Hermeneutics: Confessional Principles and Practical Applications*, Occasional Papers No. 1 of *Concordia Theological Monthly* (St. Louis: Concordia Publishing House, 1966), p. 10.
5. The German Apology says of the Roman Catholics: "dieselbige selige Lehre, das liebe, heilige Evangelium nennen sie luetherisch" (Ap XV, 44). In *Die Bekenntnisschriften der evangelisch-lutherischen Kirche* (5th rev. ed.; Goettingen: Vandenhoeck & Ruprecht, 1963), p. 305.
6. Fagerberg, p. 95.
7. *Concordia Triglotta*, ed. F. Bente (St. Louis: Concordia Publishing House, 1921), p. 121.
8. Martin Luther, *The Bondage of the Will*, trans. J. I. Packer and O. R. Johnston (Westwood, N. J.: Fleming H. Revell Company, 1957), p. 71.

Chapter 5

1. Fr. Torm, *Hermeneutik des Neuen Testaments* (Goettingen: Vandenhoeck & Ruprecht, 1930), p. 25.
2. Cf. also Ap IV, 286, where Melanchthon summarizes the above criticisms of Roman Catholic exegesis.
3. "Enthusiasm," or *Schwaermerei*, was a general label for the attempt to bypass the Word of God in man's dealings with God. Several Anabaptists, "spiritualists" like Carlstadt or Muenzer, and the radical left wing of the Reformation generally are indicated by this term.
4. Enthusiasm is condemned elsewhere in the confessions, as well. Cf. AC V; Ap IV, 66; LC IV, 15, 28; FC Ep II, 13; and FC SD II, 80.
5. Cf. FC Ep III, 7, "according to the usage of Scripture," and FC SD III, 17: "And this is the usual usage and meaning of the word in the Holy Scriptures of the Old and the New Testaments."
6. Luther's derivation of *Kirche* from the Greek is generally held to be correct, although his attempt to associate it with the Latin "curia" is probably faulty. See *Die Bekenntnisschriften der evangelisch-lutherischen Kirche* (5th rev. ed.; Goettingen: Vandenhoeck & Ruprecht, 1963), p. 656, n. 7.
7. For the prior history of this rule and its significance in Luther's thought, see F. W. Farrar, *History of Interpretation* (Bampton Lectures of 1885; Grand Rapids: Baker Book House, 1961). See also Gerhard Krause, *Studien zu*

Luthers Auslegung der Kleinen Propheten (Tuebingen: J. C. B. Mohr, 1962), pp. 174—75, n. 6.

8. Ibid., pp. 327—28.
9. A. Skevington Wood, *Luther's Principles of Biblical Interpretation* (London: The Tyndale Press, 1960), pp. 24—25.
10. Farrar, p. 327.
11. Martin Luther, *Dr. M. Luther's Answer to the Superchristian, Superspiritual, and Superlearned Book of Goat Emser of Leipzig, with a Glance at His Comrade Murner, 1521,* trans. A. Steimle, *Works of Martin Luther* (Philadelphia: A. J. Holman Company, 1930), III, 350. For Luther's distinction between *sententia generalis et specialis* and his understanding of the *scopus* of the text, see Krause, pp. 213—23 and 241—60.
12. Philipp Melanchthon, "De elementis rhetorices," *Corpus Reformatorum,* ed. Carolus Gottlieb Bretschneider, XIII (Halle: C. A. Schwetschke and Son, 1846), col. 472.
13. Ibid., col. 468.
14. Ibid., col. 469.
15. "Nun zeugen alle Umbstaende der Einsetzung dieses Abendmahls, dass diese Wort unsers Herrn und Heilands Jesu Christi, so an sich selbst einfaeltig, deutlich, klar, fest und unzweifelhaftig sein, anders nicht dann in ihrer gewoehntlichen, eigentlichen und gemeinen Deutung koennen und sollen verstanden werden," *Bekenntnisschriften,* p. 987.
16. Luther gives this advice for postulating figures of speech in Holy Scripture: "Rather let this be our conviction: that no 'implication' or 'figure' may be allowed to exist in any passage of Scripture unless such be required by some obvious feature of the words and the absurdity of their plain sense, as offending against an article of faith. Everywhere we should stick to just the simple, natural meaning of the words, as yielded by the rules of grammar and the habits of speech that God has created among men. . . . All 'figures' should rather be avoided, as being the quickest poison, when Scripture itself does not absolutely require them." In *The Bondage of the Will,* trans. J. I. Packer and O. R. Johnston (Westwood, N. J.: Fleming H. Revell Company, 1957), pp. 191—92.
17. "Diese zwei Gepot sind fast den Jueden sonderlich gegeben, wiewohl sie uns dennoch auch zum Teil betreffen," *Bekenntnisschriften,* p. 633.
18. Cf. Ap XXIV, 56, where it is stated that "by analogy [*similitudine*]" Old Testament sacrifices can be said to have merited "civil reconciliation."

Chapter 6

1. Karl Holl, "Luthers Bedeutung fuer den Fortschritt der Auslegungskunst," *Gesammelte Aufsaetze zur Kirchengeschichte,* I, *Luther* (Tuebingen: J. C. B. Mohr, 1927), 559.
2. Ibid., pp. 559—60.
3. See F. Kropatscheck, *Das Schriftprinzip der lutherischen Kirche,* I, *Die Vorgeschichte: Das Erbe des Mittelalters* (Leipzig: n. p., 1905), 448—60, for the use of this principle by Luther's predecessors.
4. This is suggested by Fr. Torm, *Hermeneutik des Neuen Testaments* (Goettingen: Vandenhoeck & Ruprecht, 1930), p. 229.
5. W. H. Schmidt and K. Schornbaum, eds., *Die Fraenkischen Bekenntnisse. Eine Vorstufe der Augsburgischen Konfession,* publ. by Landeskirchenrat der evang.-luth. Kirche in Bayern (Munich: Chr. Kaiser Verlag, 1930), p. 223.
6. Ibid., p. 217.
7. Ibid., p. 222.
8. Ibid., p. 232.
9. Ibid., pp. 16—20, for Schmidt's comments. Holsten Fagerberg characterizes

152

the Ansbach attitude toward Scripture as "a purely literal attitude to the Bible," in *A New Look at the Lutheran Confessions (1529—1537)*, trans. Gene J. Lund (St. Louis: Concordia Publishing House, 1972), p. 42.

10. Fagerberg, p. 41.
11. Cited by M. Reu, *Luther and the Scriptures* (Columbus: The Wartburg Press, 1944), reprinted in *The Springfielder*, XXIV (August 1960), 10.
12. Sometimes this hermeneutical use of articles of faith is described as the "analogy of faith." This term would emphasize not only that the whole of Scripture must be kept in mind in the interpretation of any of its parts but also that the individual articles of faith are strands of the *praecipuus locus*, the doctrine of justification by grace. Furthermore, the content of the analogy of faith is determined not by creeds or other fixed summary formulations of belief but by the sure and clear passages of Holy Scripture.
13. Above, pp. 70-71.
14. Above, pp. 69-74, especially pp. 70-72.

Chapter 7

1. Edmund Schlink, *Theology of the Lutheran Confessions*, trans. P. F. Koehneke and H. J. A. Bouman (Philadelphia: Muhlenberg Press, 1961), pp. 6—11.
2. "The Lutheran Confessions and *Sola Scriptura*," in *Essays Adopted by the Commissioners of The American Lutheran Church and The Lutheran Church—Missouri Synod*, Nov. 22—23, 1964; April 19—20, 1965 (St. Louis: Concordia Publishing House, 1965), pp. 11, 17, 18.
3. *Concordia Triglotta*, ed. F. Bente (St. Louis: Concordia Publishing House, 1921), p. 121.
4. The distinction between Law and Gospel is both quantitative and functional. In some passages God is clearly speaking Law ("Thou shalt not steal"); in others He is clearly speaking Gospel ("Believe on the Lord Jesus Christ, and thou shalt be saved and thy house"). Still others can be both Law and Gospel, depending on the emphasis; e.g., "Christ died for our sins" is Law because it emphasizes the enormity of our sins, and Gospel because it shows the extent of God's redeeming love in Jesus Christ. Cf. FC Ep V, 9—10. See also Schlink, p. 135.
5. Holsten Fagerberg, *A New Look at the Lutheran Confessions (1529—1537)*, trans. Gene J. Lund (St. Louis: Concordia Publishing House, 1972), p. 38.
6. Cited at length in Chapter 5, above, pp. 84—86.
7. Fagerberg, p. 38.
8. Ibid., p. 36.
9. Gerhard Gloege, "Die Rechtfertigungslehre als hermeneutische Kategorie," *Theologische Literaturzeitung*, LXXXIX (1964), 163.
10. Above, pp. 95—98.
11. Fagerberg, p. 38.
12. Ibid., p. 36.
13. Above, p. 36.
14. Above, pp. 69—74.
15. Attention has already been called to the Christological interpretation of the Old Testament. Cf. above, pp. 72—74.
16. "Preface," *The Book of Concord*, ed. T. G. Tappert (Philadelphia: Fortress Press, 1959), p. 3.
17. Cf., e.g., AC XX, 15, 19; AC XXV, 13; Ap IV, 20, 187, 257, 285; Ap XII, 88, 95; Ap XX, 8, 10; SA III, iii, 4, 23; Tr, 44; and LC III, 89.

Chapter 8

1. For example, the use of Sunday as a day of worship (AC XXVIII, 57—60); celebration of the Lord's Supper every Sunday (Ap XV, 40; Ap XXIV, 1); the public ceremonies of the Mass and traditional liturgical forms such as the order of the lessons, prayers, and vestments (Ap XXIV, 1; AC XXVI, 40); the observance of certain holy days and festivals (AC XV, 1); and the sign of the cross (SC VII, 1; LC I, 74).
2. Cf. "Verzeichnis der Zitate aus kirchlichen und Profanschriftstellern," *Die Bekenntnisschriften der evangelisch-lutherischen Kirche* (5th rev. ed.; Goettingen: Vandenhoeck & Ruprecht, 1963), pp. 1145—55.
3. Cf. AC XXVI, 22; AC XXVII, 36; Ap XII, 143; Ap XV, 5; Ap XXVII, 23, 69; SA II, ii, 2; and SA III, xv, 1.
4. Peter Fraenkel, *Testimonia Patrum: The Function of the Patristic Argument in the Theology of Philip Melanchthon* (Geneva: Librairie E. Droz, 1961), passim.
5. Holsten Fagerberg, *A New Look at the Lutheran Confessions (1529—1537),* trans. Gene J. Lund (St. Louis: Concordia Publishing House, 1972), p. 56, has an excellent analysis of this passage.
6. Ibid., p. 58.
7. Ibid., p. 60.
8. Friedrich Brunstaedt, *Die Theologie der lutherischen Bekenntnisschriften* (Guetersloh: C. Bertelsmann Verlag, 1951), p. 26.

Chapter 9

1. Vilmos Vajta, "The Confessions of the Church as an Ecumenical Concern," *The Church and the Confessions: The Role of the Confessions in the Life and Doctrine of the Lutheran Churches,* ed. Vilmos Vajta and Hans Weissgerber (Philadelphia: Fortress Press, 1963), pp. 168—70.
2. Ibid., p. 169.
3. C. F. W. Walther, "Why Should Our Pastors, Teachers, and Professors Subscribe Unconditionally to the Symbolical Writings of Our Church," translated and condensed by Alex Wm. C. Guebert, *Concordia Theological Monthly,* XVIII (April 1947), 242.
4. Nils Alstrup Dahl comments: "For the person who allows the church's confession to direct him to biblical exegesis, the elementary task of exegesis remains the most important and the most authentic one: the precise reading of what is written." In "The Lutheran Exegete and the Confessions of His Church," *Lutheran World,* VI (June 1959), 10.

Chapter 10

1. These and other closely related issues are treated in the *Report of the Advisory Committee on Doctrine and Conciliation* (hereafter referred to as *ACDC Report),* a compendium of position papers and responses released in 1976. This committee was established with the express purpose of identifying the difficulties challenging The Lutheran Church—Missouri Synod. See especially pp. 32, 36-37, 46. The present author has addressed some of these matters elsewhere. See "Confessional Biblical Interpretation: Some Basic Principles," in *Studies in Lutheran Hermeneutics,* ed. John Reumann, in collaboration with Samuel H. Nafzger and Harold H. Ditmanson (Philadelphia: Fortress Press, 1979), pp. 189—213; "The Church Under the Scriptures" in *The Nature and Function of Holy Scripture,* essays delivered at the Theological Convocation held at Concordia Seminary, St. Louis, April 14—18, 1975, and distributed by Concordia Publishing House, St. Louis, pp. 24—43; and finally

an abbreviated version of this volume (bearing the same title) in *Aspects of Biblical Hermeneutics: Confessional Principles and Practical Applications, Concordia Theological Monthly,* Occasional Papers No. 1, 1966, pp. 21—47. Material drawn directly from these essays is not cited again in the following notes.

2. Carl E. Braaten, *History and Hermeneutics,* in *New Directions in Theology Today,* ed. William Hordern (Philadelphia: The Westminster Press, 1966), II, 52.

3. Edgar Krentz, *Biblical Studies Today: A Guide to Current Issues and Trends* (St. Louis: Concordia Publishing House, 1966), p. 20.

4. Ibid.

5. Quoted in Samuel H. Nafzger, "Scripture and Word of God," in *Studies in Lutheran Hermeneutics,* p. 109.

6. Edgar Krentz, *The Historical-Critical Method* (Philadelphia: Fortress Press, 1975), p. 19.

7. Warren A. Quanbeck, "The Bible," in *Theology in the Life of the Church,* ed. Robert W. Bertram (Philadelphia: Fortress Press, 1963), p. 33.

8. Ibid.

9. Ralph A. Bohlmann, "The Position of the LCMS on the Basis for Fellowship," in *The Function of Doctrine and Theology in Light of the Unity of the Church,* distributed in 1978 by the Division of Theological Studies, Lutheran Council in the USA, p. 36.

10. See *Gospel and Scripture: The Interrelationship of the Material and Formal Principles in Lutheran Theology,* A Report of the Commission on Theology and Church Relations, The Lutheran Church—Missouri Synod, November, 1972, pp. 20—21.

11. Bohlmann, "The Position of the LCMS on the Basis for Fellowship," p. 36. We must hasten to add that one's faith does not *establish* the authority of Scripture; Scripture *is* inherently authoritative simply because it is the speech of God, whether man recognizes it or not.

12. Paul G. Bretscher, *After the Purifying* (River Forest, Illinois: Lutheran Education Association, 1975), p. 19.

13. Ibid., p. 77.

14. *Faithful to Our Calling, Faithful to Our Lord,* Part I: A Witness to Our Faith (St. Louis: Concordia Seminary, 1972), p. 23.

15. *ACDC Report,* pp. 38, 49.

16. Ibid., pp. 33, 36, 45.

17. Ibid.

18. Herbert J. A. Bouman has demonstrated the confessional identification of Scripture with Word of God in a painstaking (unpublished) study entitled "Source Material on 'The Word of God in the Lutheran Confessions.'" Bouman indicates that the phrase "Word of God" is equated with Scripture at least 77 times in the Lutheran confessional documents.

19. See David Kelsey, *The Use of Scripture in Recent Theology* (Philadelphia: Fortress Press, 1975), p. 30. Kelsey notes that "one basic distinction to be made among different notions of 'authority' is the distinction between understanding authority functionally and understanding it as an intrinsic property of canonical writings."

20. Nafzger, pp. 108, 122—23; Kurt E. Marquart, "The Incompatibility between Historical-Critical Theology and the Lutheran Confessions," in *Studies in Lutheran Hermeneutics,* pp. 315, 319ff.

21. Krentz, *Historical-Critical Method,* p. 4.

22. Nafzger, p. 122.

23. Gerhard Maier, *The End of the Historical-Critical Method,* trans. Edwin W.

Leverenz and Rudolph F. Norden (St. Louis: Concordia Publishing House, 1977), p. 16.
24. Ibid., p. 25.
25. Ibid., pp. 16ff., 49.
26. Ibid., p. 18.
27. Ibid., p. 25.
28. Peter Stuhlmacher, *Historical Criticism and Theological Interpretation of Scripture: Toward a Hermeneutics of Consent*, trans. Roy A. Harrisville (Philadelphia: Fortress Press, 1977), p. 67.
29. Ibid., p. 59.
30. Ibid., p. 76.
31. See below, note 41, for explanation.
32. Nafzger, pp. 112—15.
33. Marquart, p. 323.
34. Robert D. Preus, "The Hermeneutics of the Formula of Concord," in *No Other Gospel: Essays in Commemoration of the 400th Anniversary of the Formula of Concord*, ed. Arnold J. Koelpin (Milwaukee: Northwestern Publishing House, 1980), p. 316.
35. Ibid., pp. 316—17.
36. Ibid. See especially FC Ep I, 9; Ep VII, 42; SD I, 3-4, 8, 60; SD II, 8, 28, 48, 87; SD VII, 42; SD XI, 3, 12.
37. Preus, p. 317.
38. This somewhat popular misconception was perhaps fostered within The Lutheran Church—Missouri Synod when its Commission on Theology and Church Relations issued a document in 1966 outlining "basic and legitimate elements of the so-called historical-critical method" (see *A Lutheran Stance Toward Contemporary Biblical Studies*, p. 9). Although this language lacks precision, the listed "elements" are not in and of themselves subversive of Biblical authority. In fact, the document elsewhere seeks to guard against such subversion.
39. Krentz, *Historical-Critical Method*, p. 42.
40. Ibid., p. 61.
41. Ernst Troeltsch formulated the principles of historical criticism in his essay "On Historical and Dogmatic Method in Theology" (1898). The historical method brings together three principles: (1) the principle of methodological doubt or criticism, which means that history only achieves probability; (2) the principle of analogy which makes present events and experiences the criteria for determining what probably happened in the past. Analogy maintains the similarity of all events, so that one can evaluate the probability of Biblical accounts on the basis of their presence or absence in contemporary life; (3) the principle of correlation or mutual interdependence wherein all historical events are so interrelated that a change in a given event requires a corresponding change in its causes and effects. Historical explanation is based on this sequence of cause and effect, and, as practiced by Troeltsch and his consistent followers, this principle eliminates both salvation history and the miraculous. See Krentz, *Historical-Critical Method* p. 55; Anthony C. Thiselton, *The Two Horizons: New Testament Hermeneutics and Philosophical Description* (Grand Rapids: William B. Eerdmans Publishing Company, 1980), pp. 69—74.
42. Marquart, p. 318.
43. Richard N. Soulen, *Handbook of Biblical Criticism*, 2nd edition (Atlanta: John Knox Press, 1981), pp. 87—88.
44. Van A. Harvey, *The Historian and the Believer: The Morality of Historical*

Knowledge and Christian Belief (New York: The Macmillan Company, 1969), p. 42.
45. Ibid.
46. Marquart, p. 319.
47. Krentz, *Biblical Studies Today*, p. 19; *Historical-Critical Method*, pp. 62—63.
48. Krentz, *Historical-Critical Method*, p. 63.
49. *Faithful to Our Calling, Faithful to Our Lord*, Part I, p. 41.
50. It was taken for granted by the confessional fathers that there is no human standard which can be used to sit in judgment on the Scriptures and pronounce them wrong. The Preface to the *Book of Concord* frequently describes the Word of God as "pure," "infallible," "unadulterated," or "unalterable." Because we know that "God does not lie" and that "God's Word cannot err," Luther advises: "Believe the Scriptures. They will not lie to you" (LC IV, 57; V, 76). The Formula of Concord urges us "to abide by the revealed Word which cannot and will not deceive us" (FC Ep XI, 14). For other examples of such expressions, see above, pp. 44—45.
51. *Gospel and Scripture*, CTCR Report, pp. 10, 12.
52. Marquart, p. 326.
53. *ACDC Report*, p. 11.
54. Marquart, p. 326.
55. Robert D. Preus, "Confessional Subscription," in *Evangelical Directions for the Lutheran Church*, ed. Erich H. Kiehl and Waldo J. Werning (Chicago: The Lutheran Congress, 1970), p. 44.
56. Horace D. Hummel, "The Outside Limits of Lutheran Confessionalism in Contemporary Biblical Interpretation," *The Springfielder*, XXXV, No. 2 (October, 1971), p. 107.

Bibliography

Primary Sources

Die Bekenntnisschriften der evangelisch-lutherischen Kirche. 5th rev. ed. Goettingen: Vandenhoeck & Ruprecht, 1963.

The Book of Concord, ed. T. G. Tappert. Philadelphia: Fortress Press, 1959.

Concordia Triglotta, ed. and trans. F. Bente. St. Louis: Concordia Publishing House, 1921.

Secondary Sources

The American Lutheran Church. "Constitution of The American Lutheran Church," *Documents of Lutheran Unity in America,* ed. Richard C. Wolf. Philadelphia: Fortress Press, 1966. Pp. 531—538.

Bohlmann, Ralph A. "The Church Under the Scriptures," *The Nature and Fuction of Holy Scripture.* St. Louis: Concordia Publishing House, 1975. Pp. 24—43.

———. "The Position of the LCMS on the Basis for Fellowship," *The Function of Doctrine and Theology in Light of the Unity of the Church.* Distributed in 1978 by the Division of Theological Studies, Lutheran Council in the U.S.A. Pp. 32—39.

Bouman, Herbert J. A. "Some Thoughts on the Theological Presuppositions for a Lutheran Approach to the Scriptures," *Aspects of Biblical Hermeneutics: Confessional Principles and Practical Applications.* Occasional Papers No. 1 of *Concordia Theological Monthly.* St. Louis: Concorida Publishing House, 1966. Pp. 2—20.

———. "Source Material on 'The Word of God in the Lutheran Confessions.'" N.p., n.d.

Braaten, Carl E. *History and Hermeneutics,* in *New Directions in Theology Today,* ed. William Hordern. Philadelphia: The Westminster Press, 1966.

Bretscher, Paul G. *After the Purifying.* River Forest, Illinois: Lutheran Education Association, 1975.

Brunstaedt, Friedrich. *Die Theologie der lutherischen Bekenntnisschriften.* Guetersloh: C. Bertelsmann Verlag, 1951.

Chemnitz, Martin. Concerning the Interpretation of the Scripture," *Examination of the Council of Trent.* Part I, trans. Fred Kramer. St. Louis: Concordia Publishing House, 1971. Pp. 207—16.

A Comparative Study of Varying Contemporary Approaches to Biblical Interpretation. A Report of the Commission on Theology and Church Relations, The Lutheran Church—Missouri Synod, 1973.

159

"Constitution of the Lutheran Council in the United States of America," *Convention Workbook (Reports and Overtures)*. 46th Regular Convention, "The Lutheran Church—Missouri Synod, Detroit, Michigan, June 16—26, 1965. St. Louis: Concordia Publishing House, 1965. Pp. 44—47.

Dahl, Nils Alstrup. "The Lutheran Exegete and the Confessions of His Church," *Lutheran World*, VI (June 1959), 2—10.

Echternach, Helmut. "Schriftprinzip und Bekenntnis," *Evangelisch-lutherische Kirchenzeitung*, V (Feb. 15, 1951), 38—42.

Elert, Werner. *The Structure of Lutheranism*, trans. Walter A. Hansen. St. Louis: Concordia Publishing House, 1962.

Fagerberg, Holsten. *A New Look at the Lutheran Confessions*, trans. Gene J. Lund. St. Louis: Concordia Publishing House, 1972.

Faithful to Our Calling, Faithful to Our Lord, Part I: A Witness to Our Faith. St. Louis: Concordia Seminary, 1972.

Farrar, F. W. *History of Interpretation*. Bampton Lectures of 1885. Grand Rapids: Baker Book House, 1961.

Fraenkel, Peter. *Testimonia Patrum: The Function of the Patristic Argument in the Theology of Philip Melanchthon*. Geneva: Libraire E. Droz, 1961.

Gloege, Gerhard. "Die Rechtfertigungslehre als hermeneutische Kategorie," *Theologische Literaturzeitung*, LXXXIX (March 1964), 161—76.

Gospel and Scripture: The Interrelationship of the Material and Formal Principles in Lutheran Theology. A Report of the Commission on Theology and Church Relations, The Lutheran Church—Missouri Synod, 1972.

Habel, Norman. *The Form and Meaning of the Fall Narrative: A Detailed Analysis of Genesis 3*. St. Louis: Concordia Seminary Print Shop, 1965.

Harvey, Van A. *The Historian and the Believer: The Morality of Historical Knowledge and Christian Belief*. New York: The Macmillan Company, 1969.

Hermann, Rudolf. *Von der Klarheit der Heiligen Schrift: Untersuchungen und Eroerterungen ueber Luthers Lehre von der Schrift in De servo arbitrio*. Berlin: Evangelische Verlagsanstalt, 1958.

Holl, Karl. "Luthers Bedeutung Fuer den Fortschritt der Auslegungskunst," *Gesammelte Aufsaetze zur Kirchengeschichte. I. Luther*. 6th ed. Tuebingen: J. C. B. Mohr, 1927. Pp. 544—82.

Hummel, Horace D. "The Outside Limits of Lutheran Confessionalism in Contemporary Biblical Interpretation," *The Springfielder*, XXXV (September 1971), 103—25.

The Inspiration of Scripture. A Report of the Commission on Theology and Church Relations, The Lutheran Church—Missouri Synod, 1975.

Kelly, J. N. D. *Early Christian Creeds*. 2d ed. London: Longmans, Green, and Co., Ltd., 1960.

Kelsey, David. *The Use of Scripture in Recent Theology*. Philadelphia: Fortress Press, 1975.

Krause, Gerhard. *Studien zu Luthers Auslegung der Kleinen Propheten. Beitraege zur historischen Theologie,* XXXIII, ed. Gerhard Ebeling. Tuebingen: J. C. B. Mohr, 1962.

Krentz, Edgar. *Biblical Studies Today: A Guide to Current Issues and Trends.* St. Louis: Concordia Publishing House, 1966.

———. *The Historical-Critical Method.* Philadelphia: Fortress Press, 1975.

Kropatscheck, Friedrich. *Das Schriftprinzip der lutherischen Kirche,* I. Leipzig: A. Deichert, 1904.

Ladd, George Eldon, *The New Testament and Criticism.* Grand Rapids: William B. Eerdmans Publishing Company, 1967.

Linss, Wilhelm C. "Biblical Interpretation in the Formula of Concord," *The Symposium on Seventeenth Century Lutheranism.* I. St. Louis, 1962. Pp. 118—35.

Luther, Martin. *The Bondage of the Will,* trans. J. I. Packer and O. R. Johnston. Westwood, N.J.: Fleming H. Revell Company, 1957.

———. *Dr. M. Luther's Answer to the Superchristian, Superspiritual, and Superlearned Book of Goat Emser of Leipzig, with a Glance at His Comrade Murner,* 1521, trans. A. Steimle. *Works of Martin Luther.* III. Philadelphia: A. J. Holman Company, 1930. Pp. 307—401.

The Lutheran Church in America. *Constitution and By-Laws, Lutheran Church in America, Including Amendments to By-Laws Adopted at the 1964 Convention of the Church.* Philadelphia: Board of Publication, Lutheran Church in America, n.d.

"The Lutheran Confessions and Sola Scriptura," *Essays Adopted by the Commissioners of The American Lutheran Church and The Lutheran Church—Missouri Synod,* Nov. 22—23, 1964; April 19—20, 1965. St. Louis: Concordia Publishing House, 1965. Pp. 11—19.

A Lutheran Stance Toward Contemporary Biblical Studies. A Report of the Commission on Theology and Church Relations, The Lutheran Church—Missouri Synod, 1966.

The Lutheran World Federation. *Proceedings of the Fourth Assembly of the Lutheran World Federation.* Helsinki, July 30 to August 11, 1963. Berlin und Hamburg: Lutherisches Verlagshaus, 1965.

Maier, Gerhard. *The End of the Historical-Critical Method,* trans. Edwin W. Leverenz and Rudolph F. Norden. St. Louis: Concordia Publishing House, 1977.

Mayer, F. E. *The Religious Bodies of America.* 4th ed. St. Louis: Concordia Publishing House, 1961.

Melanchthon, Philipp. "De elementis rhetorices," *Corpus Reformatorum,* XIII, ed. Carolus Gottlieb Bretschneider. Halle: C. A. Schwetschke and Son, 1835. Cols. 417—506.

Montgomery, John Warwick, ed. *Crisis in Lutheran Theology.* 2 vols. Grand Rapids: Baker Book House, 1967.

Mueller, E. F. Karl, ed. *Die Bekenntnisschriften der reformierten Kirche.* Leipzig: A. Deichert'sche Verlagsbuchhandlung, 1903.

"The Order for the Ordination of a Minister," *The Lutheran Liturgy.* St. Louis: Concordia Publishing House, n.d. Pp. 106—07.

Piepkorn, Arthur Carl. "The Position of the Church and Her Symbols," in "Essays on the Inspiration of Scripture," *Concordia Theolgical Monthly,* XXV (October 1954), 738—42.

————. "Suggested Principles for a Hermeneutics of the Lutheran Symbols," *Concordia Theological Monthly,* XXIX (January 1958), 1—24.

Preus, Robert D. "Confessional Subscription," *Evangelical Directions for the Lutheran Church,* ed. Erich H. Kiehl and Waldo J. Werning. Chicago: The Lutheran Congress, 1970. Pp. 43—52.

————. The Hermeneutics of the Formula of Concord," *No Other Gospel: Essays in Commemoration of the 400th Anniversary of the Formula of Concord,* ed. Arnold J. Koelpin. Milwaukee: Northwestern Publishing House, 1980. Pp. 309—35.

Quanbeck, Warren A. "The Bible," *Theology in the Life of the Church,* ed. Robert W. Bertram. Philadelphia: Fortress Press, 1963. Pp. 22—39.

Report of the Advisory Committee on Doctrine and Conciliation. St. Louis: Concordia Publishing House, 1975.

Report of the Synodical President to The Lutheran Church—Missouri Synod, issued September 1, 1972.

Reu, M. *Luther and the Scriptures.* Columbus, Ohio: The Wartburg Press, 1944. Reprinted in *The Springfielder,* XXIV (August 1960).

Reuman, John, ed., in collaboration with Samuel H. Nafzger and Harold H. Ditmanson. *Studies in Lutheran Hermeneutics.* Philadelphia: Fortress Press, 1979.

Roloff, Juergen. "The Interpretation of Scripture in Article IV of Melanchthon's Apology of the Augsburg Confession," *Lutheran World,* VIII (June 1961), 47—63.

Schlink, Edmund. *Theology of the Lutheran Confessions,* trans. P. F. Koehneke and H. J. A. Bouman. Philadelphia: Fortress Press, 1961.

Schmidt, Wilhelm F., and K. Schornbaum, eds. *Die Fraenkischen Bekenntnisse. Eine Vorstufe der Augsburgischen Konfession.* Publ. by Landeskirchenrat der evang.-luth. Kirche in Bayern. Munich: Chr. Kaiser Verlag, 1930.

Schroeder, H. J., trans. *Canons and Decrees of the Council of Trent.* St. Louis: B. Herder Book Co., 1950.

Soulen, Richard N. *Handbook of Biblical Criticism.* 2d Edition. Atlanta: John Knox Press, 1981.

A Statement of Scriptural and Confessional Principle. Study Edition. Issued by The Commission on Theology and Church Relations, 1972.

Stuhlmacher, Peter. *Historical Criticism and Theological Interpretation of Scripture: Towards a Hermeneutics of Consent,* trans. Roy A. Harrisville. Philadelphia: Fortress Press, 1977.

Thiselton, Anthony C. *The Two Horizons: New Testament Hermeneutics and Philosophical Description.* Grand Rapids: William B. Eerdmans Publishing Company, 1980.

Torm, Fr. *Hermeneutik des Neuen Testaments.* Goettingen: Vandenhoeck & Ruprecht, 1930.

Vajta, Vilmos, and Hans Weissgerber, eds. *The Church and the Confessions: The Role of the Confessions in the Life and Doctrine of the Lutheran Churches.* Philadelphia: Fortress Press, 1963.

Walther, C. F. W. "Why Should Our Pastors, Teachers, and Professors Subscribe Unconditionally to the Symbolical Writings of Our Church," trans. and condensed by Alex Wm. C. Guebert, *Concordia Theological Monthly*, XVIII (April 1947), 241—53.

Walther, Wilhelm. *Das Erbe der Reformation im Kampf der Gegenwart.* I. Leipzig: A. Deichert'sche Verlagsbuchhandlung, 1903.

Wood, A. Skevington. *Luther's Principles of Biblical Interpretation.* London: The Tyndale Press, 1960.